CwG

When Everything Changes, Change Everything

WORKBOOK & STUDY GUIDE

A companion to the groundbreaking text that introduces a new combination of modern psychology and contemporary spirituality in the WECCE TECHNOLOGY, based on the messages in Conversations with God .

NEALE DONALD WALSCH

A publication of
Spiritual Legacies – $12.95

CwG

Table of Contents

Introduction

Introduction

I am glad that you came to this document because it says to me that you are a serious student of the WECCE material.

As you may know, *When Everything Changes, Change Everything* is a condensation of the life-changing messages in the *Conversations with God* series of books. That series covered over 3,000 pages in 9 texts. WECCE has condensed and congealed that material into 300 pages in a single book. It offers two remarkable tools that combine modern psychology and contemporary spirituality: The Mechanics of the Mind and the System of the Soul. The text provides a detailed explanation of how the Mind works and how the Soul functions, as well as how to use these tools conjointly in your everyday life.

The Workbook & Study Guide you are now reading **takes WECCE one step further**, moving into deep discussion around the WECCE Promises made in the original text. In this exploration I will touch on many of the things that I said in the book itself, but **add to and expand on** what was said there, offering an opportunity to dive more deeply into both the meaning and the nuance of the original material.

You will recall that in the text I said I believe that by using the WECCE Technology you will be able to change Fear into Excitement, Worry into Wonder, Expectation into Anticipation, Resistance into Acceptance, Disappointment into Detachment, Enragement into Engagement, Addiction into Preference, Requirement into Contentment, Judgment into Observation, Sadness into Happiness, Thought into Presence, Reaction into Response, and a Time of Turmoil into a Time of Peace.

Those are mighty big promises. Yet I believe they are promises that can be kept. Much will depend on you, however. You will have to be committed to the process. And so the biggest promise is a promise you will have to make to yourself. You are being invited here to resolve to pay much closer attention to how you are living your life; to how you are engaging your Mind—and how you are allowing your Mind to engage you.

AND...to how you are connecting with your Soul. For connecting with your Soul on a daily basis is at the heart of the WECCE Technology, and makes possible the WECCE Promises.

I am also inviting you here to pledge to make the Nine Changes That Can Change Everything. For your review, those Nine Changes are:

1. Change your decision to "go it alone"
2. Change your choice of emotions
3. Change your choice of thoughts
4. Change your choice of truths
5. Change your idea about Change Itself
6. Change your idea about why Change occurs.
7. Change your idea about future Change
8. Change your idea about life
9. Change your identity

The WECCE text itself discusses these nine changes thoroughly, so we will not go into them in detail here. What we *will* do is take a close look at those 13 promises. Can the WECCE Technology really do those things? I believe it can, and we will explore those promises here, one by one. But first, this warning: **You cannot and will not make much sense of this Workbook if you have not read *When Everything Changes, Change Everything* from cover to cover. The languaging and the references here assume that you have done that.** This document is meant to be an *adjunct*, not a stand-alone text. It is important to encounter it in that context.

Chapter One: Changing Fear into Excitement

Conversations with God says that everything begins with either Love or Fear. Every thought, every word, every action. Nothing opens us wider to the wonders of life than Love, and nothing paralyzes us faster than Fear.

Yet Fear is a fiction.

I want to say that again, because it is the basis of everything you need to understand as you move through your life, and everything you need to know as you seek to change Fear into Excitement.

I said that *Fear is a fiction.*

It is not real.

It is something you are making up in your Mind.

It is a false emotion; a counterfeit feeling; a distortion, rooted in a deep misunderstanding.

> **Fear is a fiction. Is it not real. It is something you are making up in your Mind.**

In truth, there is only one emotion, there is only one energy, there is only One Thing That Is. "All things are One Thing," say *Conversations with God.* "There is only One Thing, and all things are part of the One Thing That Is."

Emotion is nothing more than e*nergy In motion.* Hence: E+motion. There is only one Energy, thus, there is only one Energy in Motion all the time. The human word we have given for that one Emotion is Love. That is why *Conversations with God* says: "Love is all there is."

If this is true (and it is), then Fear, as a separate emotion, does not exist. It may exist as an *experience*, but not as an emotion.

Is this true? Is this possible?

The experience of Fear is the emotion of Love, distorted. That is another important statement. It, too, deserves repeating.

The experience of Fear is the emotion of Love, distorted.

All Fear is an expression of Love.

What? Can this be *true?*

Yes. It can be, and it is.

Once you understand this, you will know how to deal with Fear—-because, ironically, *you will no longer be afraid of it.* It is your *fear* of Fear that give Fear its power. If you embrace Fear, welcome it, hold it close, it *has* no power. You literally *love it to death.*

This is, in short, how you are going to turn your Fear into Excitement. And this process is all a function of the Mind.

It is your Mind that turns Love into Fear, and it is your Mind that will turn Fear into Excitement. Your Mind can turn *anything into anything!* That is its magic. That is the Magic of the Mind.

Okay, let's get to some clarifications; let's move to some deeper understandings.

I have said, "All Fear is an expression of Love." How can this be possible? you may ask. How can this be true?

Well, let's look at that.

If you did not love yourself, would you be afraid of anything happening to you?

If you did not love life, would you be afraid of losing it? (People who hate life---people who, for instance, are in abject misery or unremitting pain---are not afraid of losing life at all. In fact, they welcome it.)

If you did not love others, would you be afraid that they might fall into danger?

No. You would not care, you would not worry. Only Love causes you to be afraid. Absent Love, Fear is not.

So you can know with great certainty that if you are in fear, you are in love. The trick is to not let the love that you feel turn into the fear that you are very able to experience. You can turn this trick by using the Mechanics of the Mind.

That famous acronym

So we begin with this clarity: Fear is **F**alse **E**vidence **A**ppearing **R**eal. That is a famous acronym that everyone in the so-called New Age Community has heard over and over again. Yet my experience has been that very few spiritual teachers explain it fully. Very few tell us what the false evidence *is* that is looking so real.

This false evidence is so powerful that it produces a thought—-a thought that is then made real.

I have said that your Mind can turn that which is not real into that which is real, and this is true. Your Mind is able to do this because it does not deal with what is *really* real, it deals with what you *think* is real. Indeed, it *tells* you what to think. It does this all the time. It is *supposed* to do this. *That is its function*.

No one ever explained this to me in school. No one told me this in church. My parents never said anything about it to me at home. *I never got this information anywhere.*

Your *Mind* is *telling you what to think*, based on the evidence at hand.

I was raised knowing nothing of this not because the adults around me didn't want to tell me about it, but they didn't know it themselves. Unless you took a course in clinical psychology, you could spend an entire lifetime knowing nothing about the Mechanics of the Mind.

I have never taken such a course, so I had to find out another way—-through the Wisdom of the Soul. The process by which one learns (more accurately, *remembers*) what is "so" through accessing the Wisdom of the Soul will be discussed in this workbook later. For now it is sufficient for us to simply know this: We are all living in an Illusion.

As I am fond of saying (and so you may have heard this from me before…), we have fallen down the rabbit hole, and the Mad Hatter is sitting in front of us pouring tea into a cup with no bottom, all the while telling us that what is "so" is *not* so, and that what is "not so" is *so*.

And we believe him.

We believe him.

What the Mad Hatter never said

What we were not told by that rascal in the rabbit hole is that *nothing we see is real*. The "evidence" that is "false" is the *appearance* of things.

That's it! *That's the false evidence.*

When we look at something, we think we are seeing what we are looking at. Yet we are not seeing what we are looking at, we are seeing *our interpretation* of what we are looking at. That is why two people can look at the same thing and see *two entirely different things.*

(I'll never forget how shocked I was when I read an article about myself in *People* magazine. In the story it said, "Walsch lives in a mansion on the outskirts of Ashland, in Southern Oregon." I lived at the time in a three-bedroom home with a den on the lowest level and a two-car garage that I had converted into an office. The reporter and I were looking at the exact same house. I never thought of it as a "mansion.")

We have been thrown into an environment (the Realm of the Physical) in which everything exists *relationally.* That is, things appear to be what they appear to be because of the relationship they hold to other things.

The only place where we can see things in their entirety, and thus Know Completely, is in the Realm of the Absolute. This realm can only be accessed by being there. Yet this is not as difficult as it sounds, for there is a part of us that IS there, *all the time.* We call that part of us The Soul.

> We have forgotten who we are. We have forgotten what is so.

The Soul lives in *all realms eternally*.

The Mind lives only in the Realm of the Relative.

Because of this, the Mind's perspective is *extremely limited.* It is important to understand this. It is more than "important." It is vital.

It is also good to understand that the Mind's limited perspective is *not a handicap.* The Mind was *intended* to hold a limited perspective, for it is this limited view that allows us to move through the experience of physicality and do what we came here to do.

Consider a horse, moving through a busy street in a hectic city. Without blinders the horse cannot make it. He must be made to focus only on what is directly ahead of him. Remove the blinders and the horse will rear up in panic, all from a single cause: *too much data.*

It is the same with humans.

Our bodies and minds are the horses of the Soul, carrying it through this hectic environment. Memory lapses are our blinders.

We have forgotten Who We Are. We have forgotten What Is So. We *must* if we are to get through this busy street. We don't dare take the blinders off, because then we would see everything—-and the Mind is incapable of analyzing all that data at once.

Ultimate Reality is *incalculable.*

Yet this does not mean that we cannot look at parts of it, one part at a time. We can do this with our blinders on, simply by turning our head, focusing away from one thing and onto another.

That is what "transformation" is all about. It is about looking away from one thing and toward another.

In physical life, our blinders never come off, *but we can look wherever we want to look.*

This is what Masters understand, and this is what Students are striving to learn.

So judge not by appearances

So we see that the false evidence that appears real is the appearance of things. I should now like to give you a concrete example. Let us consider the illusion of *speed.* Speed is simply an appearance. There is actually no such thing as *speed* except in relative terms.

We say that the train is going fifty miles an hour, and thus, it is moving very fast. Yet when observed from the window of a train on the next track that is also going fifty miles an hour, it seems to be not moving at all. This is because, *relative to each other*, the two trains are *not* moving. Indeed, you could pass a glass of wine from the window of one to the window of the other without spilling a drop.

But wait. It gets even more interesting. If the second train is moving at fifty-*five* miles an hour, the first train will appear to be moving *backward.* In which case, seeing is *not* believing.

So much for the reliability of what your Mind is telling you.

Limited data

As I have explained, none of this is the Mind's "fault." It is working with that limited data I spoke of. And that's *as it should be*, that's okay---unless we think *that's all the data there is.*

The problem in our world is, we do. Most people do. We think that the Mind's data is the *sum total* of all the data that exists about life.

This is, of course, not true---a point to which we will return later. For now, let us consider the problem.

Train 'A' now seems to be moving backward, even though it is going fifty miles an hour in the same direction as Train 'B'. And if we have a friend on Train A who we hope will reach the same destination as us at the same time, we will suddenly be in Fear that *he will never get there.*

Our Fear is based on *the appearance of things*. It has nothing to do with Ultimate Reality.

How to understand what is really true here? Simple. Judge not by appearances. *Get more data.*

As carefully explained in the WECCE text, the Mind comes to its conclusions about what it is seeing based on the all of its accumulated Past Data. If the person viewing this Train Event is not an experienced traveler, he will have *no way of knowing* that the first train is not moving backward. Only if he has information stored in his Past Data that tells him *what is so* about *speed* will he be able to understand that the first train is not going backward at all and is, in fact, moving in the same direction as the second, but that the second train is simply slowing pulling away.

> **Education is good.**
> **Expansion is better.**

We see, then, that the reality we experience is based on the data we hold. Wait. Is that important enough to repeat? I think so. I said...*The reality we experience is based on the data we hold.*

Reality and data are intrinsically tied in what I fondly call the Mind Field. This is the same as a Mine Field. If we aren't careful about where we are going, it could be dangerous.

The Mind cannot reach before 'before'

Always remember this: the Mind has nothing to *go on* except what *went on.* It can only consider what has occurred before. And the Mind's "before" stretches back all the way to the months prior to our birth (which is miraculous enough)...but it cannot reach *before that.* It cannot reach "before Before."

Did I state that clearly? What I am saying is that the Mind cannot reach back before the first "before" it ever stored. And it didn't start storing data until it began functioning. So that data is limited to what the Mind has collected from the first moments of its activation. As for the Time that existed before your Mind began functioning, that Time may as well never have existed.

Trains have been going faster than one another down parallel tracks long before you were born---but if you've never encountered such an Event, it might as well *never have happened before.*

That's where history books come in---except that history is also based on misperceptions!

There are two ways to overcome this limitation of the Mind. These are: *Education* and *Expansion.*

We can educate ourselves about the Time Before, or we can expand our consciousness to include data about the Time Before.

Education is good. Expansion is better.

The problem with education is that it limits the Mind's Data to the Data that Other Minds have collected through the years. This is not all bad, and indeed, it is how we have managed to survive through all these many years. Yet as I have just noted, the data of others is limited as well. So if we wish to do more than simply survive; if we wish to *evolve*, we are going to have to not merely educate the Mind, but expand it.

This is the choice that is always before us: Survive or Evolve. If we choose the first, we will take one course of action. If we choose the second, we will often take another.

Evolution does not necessarily involve survival of your present physical form. The evolution of the Soul sometimes invites decisions and actions that might place your present physical form in some danger. There is no way that the Mind is going to allow you to do that. Not if you are limiting the Mind's considerations to the data that it has collected since the first moments of its functioning (what I call the Mind's "activation"). We need to add to the Mind's data if we expect the Mind to give up its main mission---which is to ensure the survival of the Body.

And we are going to have to add to that data not simply by grabbing data from a More Distant Past, but also access data from a Past Before Past. From a Time Before Time, if you will. We will need to consider the Data of All Time/No Time. And that is a place where the Mind, for all its ingenious functioning, cannot go. To collect data from this place, the Mind must rely on the Soul.

The basis of everything

I am going into this extensive explanation in this first chapter of the Workbook and Study Guide because this understanding forms the basis of everything else that appears in this document. It is vital that you really grasp what is being said in these early paragraphs, or little hereafter will fall into place, and you may struggle with it.

What we are discussing in this first chapter is Fear. And what I am telling you is that Fear is not real. It is a figment of your imagination. It is a distortion of the Only Thing There Is, which is Love.

I am saying that this distortion is created in your Mind, which thinks it has all the data you need in order to make it possible for the Body to survive. What the Mind does not understand is that the Body does not *have* to survive in order for the Totality That Is You to accomplish its mission.

The reason that the Mind, for all its magnificent mechanisms, does not understand this is that the Mind thinks that the Body IS the "Totality That Is You." *The Mind thinks that you are your Body.*

Again, limited data. Yet CwG tells us that your Body is not something you are, it is something you *have.* If this is true (and it is), then who is this "You" that has this Body? Is it the Mind? No. Is it the Soul? No. What I call "The Totality That Is You" is a *combination* of the Body-Mind-Soul. It is all three.

I am saying that you are a 3-part being, made up of Body, Mind, AND Soul. You are not *one* of these three parts, you are *all* of these three parts, In One.

Your Mind has no way of understanding this if it considers only the data that it has collected since the moment of its Activation. The *Soul* is the part of you where this information resides. That is the place from which I, myself, drew this data before writing it here. The data I am sharing with you now did not come from my Mind, it came from my Soul.

You can access the same data if you move from your own Mind to your own Soul. The same data exists in all souls, because all souls are one soul. There is only one Soul, and all souls are part of the One Soul There Is. You could call this One Soul "God."

Where Fear comes from

Now, your Mind does not know any of this. That is, your Mind does not know anything about Who You Really Are (an Individuation of the One Soul There Is). It imagines that you are the singular entity that is called (fill in your name here). It also imagines that this singular entity can die; it imagines that you somehow, some time, somewhere, *cannot be.*

The truth is, you cannot "not be," but the Mind does not know this. This is because the Mind has been told of a Time when "you" were not. It is aware that your "memory" only goes back as far as the Time of its Activation---but it also knows (because other Minds have collected and stored data about their experience in a physical form that we call this our "recorded history") that there was a Time Before You; there were things that were happening before you were born.

This is true. There *were* things that were happening before you were born...but there are *no* things that were happening before you *were*. Such a thing would be impossible, because you *always* were. You always were, are now, and always will be.

You could only accept this as true, you could only embrace it, if you were clear that you are not your Body, but that your Body is merely something you *have.*

Because your Mind thinks that you *are* your Body, it thinks that loss is possible, that damage is real, and that something can occur that can injure you in some way---or perhaps even end your life.

None of these things are possible, but your Mind thinks they are. And that is where Fear comes from. It is what you feel when your Mind looks at the evidence before it and assumes it to be real. It is **F**alse **E**vidence **A**ppearing **R**eal.

What is "false" in this evidence is the apparency of Who You Really Are. The Apparent Truth is that you are your Body. The Actual Truth is that you are The Totality of Your Being---Body, Mind, and Soul---and that that this Totality can *never* die, nor be hurt or damaged in any way.

Most people are experiencing life as a Case of Mistaken Identity. They imagine they are their Body. They have fallen down the rabbit hole. They have jumped into the Matrix. They think that what is happening is real. Yet it is not real. Nothing you see is real. Everything you are looking at is an illusion.

Once this is understood, Fear disappears. This is what the movie *The Matrix* was trying to show us. When the main character, Neo, understood that the whole thing was an illusion, nothing could touch him.

Of course, we say, that was only a movie…

Or was it?

Is it possible that *this* is the movie, and *that* is the reality?

Let's see how much you remember

Following is the first of several Exercises, Quizzes, Assignments, and Experiments that I have prepared for you as a means of expanding the material in *When Everything Changes, Change Everything* and bringing it closer to your on-the-ground experience.

In the first Exercise, below, I want to find out how much you have retained of what you read in the book about all that we have just been discussing. I consider WECCE one of the most important books you will ever read. But it will do you no good at all to have read it if you have not really absorbed and retained its contents. Do not feel 'bad' if the following Exercise reveals that you have not. Yet promise yourself that you will return to the WECCE text and review the writing there. It is really important that you remember and internalize this information.

If you remember what you read in the WECCE text (or elsewhere in the *Conversations with God* material), you will already know that you are not your Body, and that the "You" that you are lives forever and cannot die. Most of the world's mainstream religions also tell us that.

This chases Fear right out of your life. Or it should. For as *Conversations with God* says, "When you are not afraid of dying, you are not afraid of living." And why would you be afraid of dying if you thought you were going to live forever---and see all your loved ones while you do? (Which CwG promises.) Of course, many people *are* afraid of dying---because of what many religions tell us is going to happen to us after our death. Or *could* happen, at least, if we are not "good."

This is another whole story that the Mind has accepted as True (unless it has not), and it is from this Past Data that so many of our realities are created. These ideas, in turn, are rooted in that larger misunderstanding I have been speaking of, about who you are and why you are here. On the earth, I mean. In this present environment, in physical form. The WECCE text explains all this in the "Figure 8 Discourse." Now, let's see what you remember of that data.

Exercise 1

1. **Take out a sheet of paper and on it answer the Four Fundamental Questions of Life: Who Are You? Where are you? Why are you where you are? What are you trying to do here? Base your answers on the Figure 8 Discourse in *When Everything Changes, Change Everything,* Chap. 19: The Eternal Journey of the Soul, but *without referring to the chapter*. (The purpose of this exercise is to see what part of the information you remember and understand.)**

2. **How many realms are there in the "Kingdom of God"?**

3. **What is meant by The Realm of the Absolute?**

4. **If we "know everything" in The Realm of Knowing, why bother journeying to The Realm of the Physical?**

5. **Now go to Pg. 185 in the WECCE book and re-read Chap. 19. Check your answers against what is found in the text.**

We see now that, in the Realm of the Absolute, Love is all there is. Fear is a distorted expression of Love, growing out of the limited data of your Mind.

Getting back to that train...

Now that we have all this pulled together, let's go back to our experience of that train.

To recap: Your train, Train 'B', is on Track 2. On Track 1, which you can see out the window, is Train 'A'. When both trains were moving at the same speed, it appeared as if neither train was moving at all. But now Train 'A' has slowed down by five miles an hour, while Train 'B' continues at its present speed. It appears now as if Train 'A' is actually going *backward.*

(I experienced this same phenomenon of juxtaposed realities once, in a parking garage. The guy in the car next to me began backing out of his space. But I did not know that there was a man IN the car next to me. I was busy putting my key in the ignition and simply did not see him. So when I noticed the car next to me moving, I did not "get" that it was backing up. I thought that *I was rolling forward.* I ferociously slammed my foot on the brake---at which point my startled passenger asked me what in the hell I was doing...)

Now in our train example, if you are an inexperienced traveler, you might begin creating an interesting "reality" based on your Mind's limited data. As I showed before, you might actually be "afraid" for the people in Train 'A'. Do they know their train is going *backward?*

To reiterate, for emphasis: This fear---like my fear in the parking garage---is based on the *appearance* of things. I thought *for sure* that my car was rolling forward and was going to hit the wall. My Mind held limited data. It did not know that a man was in the car next to me, and had begun to back out.

Expanded data eliminates Fear

I know I am repeating myself here, because I want to make this point indelibly: When your Mind has limited data, it has no choice but to *work with the data it has.* If I had seen that guy in the next car, that information would have become part of my Past Data, and when the man's car began to back out, I would have *seen it for what it was.* I would have then been afraid of nothing.

> **When your Mind has limited data, it has no choice but to work with the data it has.**

When we see things as they really are, we are afraid of nothing. *And this is how we change Fear into Excitement.* We *see things as they really are.*

Yet to see things as they really are we have to be out of our Mind.

"Are you crazy??? Are you out of your mind???" people have asked me many times in my life...and I have had to say, well, *yes.* I have had to agree with them. They're right. I'm out of my Mind. Which in many cases in the best place to be.

Fear becomes Excitement when we expand the data that our Mind is considering. *We do this by moving outside of the Mind and into the Soul.*

[

Finding your way to the Soul

Yes, but how?

Well, as I said earlier, getting to the Soul is easier than you might think. It can be done in a number of ways, and you can even use your Mind to get there, which is good news, because it is very difficult to conceive of anything which the Mind rejects.

Fortunately, the human Mind has not totally rejected the notion that such a thing as the Soul could exist. This idea has been placed in the Mind by the Past Data of humanity, our history, including the information given to us by our religions, all of which speak of the "spirit" or the "soul."

So now that we know that the possibility of the Soul exists, all we have to do is find it; get in touch with it. As I said, this may be easier than you think.

The fastest way to find our path to the Soul, from my experience, is prayer or meditation. And right now I am wondering how much you remember from the WECCE text about *that*.

The purpose of the quiz at right is to see if you are doing your meditation---at least *some* form of meditation---every day. If you are not, this may be why you continue to live in Fear instead of Excitement.

Now I will answer the last question in the quiz for you. Meditation is not about emptying the Mind, it is about *focusing* the Mind. It is virtually impossible to "empty the mind." That is, to "think about nothing." It is not impossible, however, to focus the Mind---to think about something specific, but that has nothing to do with your worries, your problems, your frustrations, or anything in your everyday life.

QUIK QUIZ #1

What are the several forms of meditation described in
When Everything Changes, Change Everything?

**Which is the quickest method,
and how does it work?**

What is Walking Meditation?

**Meditation is not about emptying the Mind.
What, then, *is* it about?**

By this process you literally *get your Mind off of* what agitates you and causes you to lose your peace (and maybe even move you into Fear), and onto something that *brings* you peace ...or no emotion at all, which IS peace, defined.

In this way you *use* your Mind, rather than *lose* your Mind. So meditation is about using your Mind to *get out* of your Mind. The WECCE text offers you several powerful ways to meditate. I hope you will use them.

Another method: Soul Searching

There is another way that a person can find the path to the Soul, especially with regard to a particular life issue, and that is through "soul searching."

This is a method of searching the Soul for answers to questions that the Mind can barely contemplate. It involves a process that spontaneously emerged through me while I was facilitating a CwG Spiritual Renewal Retreat. A participant was having a difficult time resolving sadness and grief around a series of tragic events in her life. Knowing that her peace would not come from looking at these events from the standpoint of the Mind, but only from the perspective of the Soul, I began asking her some questions to see if I could coax her into taking that perspective. She answered the questions in a very clear and powerful way---and came to an almost immediate healing of her unresolved and very deep sadness.

Later in the same retreat another person, no doubt encouraged by what he saw had happening with the lady, raised his hand and told his personal story---which was even more tragic. I asked him the same questions I had asked the lady. The same thing happened. He experienced an almost immediate healing of his enormous grief.

I saw that I "had something here," and so, throughout the rest of the retreat, I used this process that I "stumbled upon." I use it constantly today. I have found that it gets to the heart of any matter very quickly. I call the process **SouLogic**. You can use the process on yourself simply by asking yourself the same questions I asked the folks in the retreat, and answering them.

the

SouLogic

Process

The **SouLogic** process surrounds the asking of six questions:

1. **Do you believe in God?**
2. **Do you believe in the existence of the human Soul?**
3. **Do you believe that the Soul is eternal and can never die?**
4. **What do you believe is the relationship between the Soul and God?**
5. **Do you believe the soul ever does anything against its will, that it doesn't want to do, or that the Soul can be victimized or damaged in any way?**
6. **What do you believe is the purpose of your Soul having experienced what it has experienced in this lifetime?**

The answers to these questions will send you on a Soul Searching that can produce direct connection between your Mind and your Soul, opening you to the Consciousness of the Soul and the Awareness that goes along with it.

This process can change people's lives in just moments, altering their reality around any life event through the *expanding of the data* in the Mind's databank.

Once you have "established contact" with your Soul on a regular basis you are on your way to changing the way you think about everything in your life---and about life itself. By connecting with your Soul and embracing the consciousness of Pure Being, you expand the databank of the Mind, bringing it information, understanding, and awareness that it has no way of retrieving from its own previously limited storehouse---*because it is not there.*

The SouLogic Process in action

Now let's see how this **SouLogic** process can work in 'real life,' helping you to change Fear into Excitement.

Let us say that a person is living in Fear of not having enough money. Now let's pretend that I am working with that person (we'll call him 'Harry') using this process. Here's how one interaction might go…

NEALE: Do you believe in God?

HARRY: Yes.

NEALE: Okay. Do you believe in the existence of the Human Soul?

HARRY: Yes.

NEALE: Do you believe that the Soul is eternal and can never die?

HARRY: Yes, I do.

NEALE: What do you believe is the relationship between the Soul and God?

HARRY: I'm not sure. I don't know.

NEALE: I see. But if you *thought* you knew, what would your answer be?

HARRY: I would think that the Soul and God are deeply connected.

NEALE: In what way?

HARRY: I'm not sure I can describe it.

NEALE: If you had to try, what would you say?

HARRY: I'd say that the Soul and God are the 'same stuff,' only God has more of it. Something like that.

NEALE: Great, I got that. Do you believe that the Soul ever does anything against its will, or can be victimized or damaged in any way?

HARRY: That's a good question. I don't know.

NEALE: I know, but if you thought you did, what would your answer be?

HARRY: I don't think so. Not really. *WE* might be able to be damaged; I mean, the human ego, but I don't think the Soul can be victimized or damaged.

NEALE: Then what do you believe is the purpose of your soul having experienced what it has experienced in this lifetime?

HARRY: I want to say 'I don't know,' but I know what you're going to tell me.

NEALE: Good, then we can go right to the answer.

Here the process participant will often give a detailed answer to the question, *Why has my Soul experienced this?* It always amazes everyone in the room, because the answer is startling in its clarity. Any thought that the participant did not have the answer is wiped out immediately.

Once the answer is clear, once the reason and the purpose of life's events is understood, Fear---with regard to that event or even future life events---evaporates, to be replaced by a new excitement for life. A person suddenly sees exactly what is going on here in this life, why things are happening the way they are happening, why things are *going* to be happening the way they are going to be happening (when though we don't know *what* is going to happen), and the wondrous perfection of it all.

Calling everything "perfect" is not the same as calling everything "wonderful." Calling a condition perfect is simply acknowledging that it exists in exact alignment with your soul's in-this-moment agenda---which may very well be to *change* the condition as a means of knowing, demonstrating, and experiencing Who You Really Are.

What a teacher once told me

I remember getting on a roller coaster when I was a kid. I was kind of scared at first, but my father convinced me that the ride was perfectly safe, that nothing bad was going to happen to me, and that I had nothing to worry about. My father had his arm around me, and there were nothing but thrills ahead of me. In that moment my Fear changed into Excitement.

Years later I was having a conversation about Fear with a spiritual teacher of mine. I told her about my roller coaster experience and she said, "So Neale, what did you learn from that?" When I paused she said, "You might have learned that from now on it could be interesting to simply *call your fears adventure.*"

That teacher changed my life with those four words: CALL YOUR FEARS ADVENTURE. And now I have a new acronym for Fear: **F**eeling **E**xcited **A**nd **R**eady.

These days when I think about things that are going to happen or that could happen, I feel that I am perfectly safe, that nothing bad is going to occur, and that I have nothing to worry about. After all, I have my Father's arms around me…

Exercise 2

1. **Think of three times in your life when you were really in fear about something. It could be an event you thought was going to happen, or an outcome that you were deeply apprehensive about, or anything at all that put you into fear.**
2. **Make a list of those three things, and in a second column next to them, write down how things actually turned out.**
3. **In a third column to the right of the second, make an entry telling in a few words how you feel about that whole experience today.**
4. **What, if anything, does this tell you about what you may fear today?**

My life is a roller coaster for sure, but I have nothing but thrills ahead, and I am excited to see what form those thrills are going to take. I also know now Who I Am, where I am, why I am where I am, and what I am trying to do here. I've answered all of those questions for myself, so I've taken a lot of the unknown out of that roller coaster. It's still fun, but it's not a mystery to me.

A final word about Fear, please. Please be clear that Fear and Caution are not the same thing. The person who looks both ways before crossing the street is not living in fear, she is simply very wise. The person who carries an umbrella on a cloudy day is not "afraid" that it will rain, he is simply being prudent.

Do not abandon Caution in the name of Fearlessness. Recklessness and Fearlessness are not synonyms. Your Mind is not your enemy. It has not given you Past Data to thwart you, but to protect you and keep you safe. It may have *limited* data, but all its data are not *useless.* Pay attention to them. But also, *expand them.* That's what we're saying here. We're not saying "ignore the Mind." We're saying, *open the Mind.* For it is as Shakespeare said:

"There are more things in heaven and earth, Horatio, than are dreamt of in your philosophy."

Chapter Two: Changing Worry into Wonder

Worry is the first cousin of Fear. It is its precursor. It is the cough before the cold, the misstep before the fall.

Worry is an announcement that you hold a belief that something other than what is best for you could happen. A person who is clear that all outcomes are perfect would never have a reason to worry.

I spent a lot of time in Chapter One of this Workbook & Study Guide laying the groundwork for how the other changes in our list of promises can be made. All involve the same approach: using the Mechanics of the Mind to our advantage rather than our disadvantage, by expanding the database of the Mind through whatever process works for us to connect with our Soul---meditation, prayer, SouLogic, etc.

That groundwork having been laid, let's look now at how we can turn worry into wonder.

Ah, sweet mystery of life...

The most wonderful part about life is not knowing how it's going to turn out. Whether we're talking the whole of one's life or some particular chapter within it, it's the *mystery* of life that holds its fascination; it's the *not knowing* that captures our imagination.

(If we "don't know" how something is going to turn out, we can "imagine" how it might---and that's easily half the fun.)

> **Worry is the first cousin of fear.**

Few of us would want to know, for instance, the exact moment that we are going to die. We may *say* that we'd like to know, but in truth, it would be more of a burden than a blessing for most of us.

Similarly, half the fun of a romance is the intrigue. If you know ahead of time that there's no doubt about the outcome, surely the experience loses some of its luster.

Having said all of that, it would seem that "worry" might not be such a bad thing. There's a very short distance between "intrigue" and "worry," after all, is there not?

Yet "worry" wears the Body and the Mind down a lot more than "intrigue." And any person would rather be "fascinated" by possibilities than "worried" about dreaded outcomes.

"It's all good," as the kids today say

Earlier I said that worry is an announcement that you hold a belief that something other than what is best for you could happen. *Lack* of worry, however, does not mean that you know exactly what is going to happen. It simply means you are clear that *no matter what* happens, it's going to be perfect.

Now that's a tough one for most people to swallow. No matter what happens, it's going to be "perfect"? *Are you kidding?* No.

All things are perfect, or they wouldn't be happening. Evolution is a process by which one thing leads to another in a way that always, always, *always* sustains life and advances the agenda of the Life Itself (which is to become More of Itself). Life always wants to produce more life.

Yet how can this be true? Is it not a fact that some things occur in life which do not sustain life, but end it? Are there not black holes in space? Are there not predators in jungles? Do not accidents occur in human life? Does not misfortune strike? Is tragedy to be made light of?

Are we to *pretend* that nothing "bad" happens and that therefore there is nothing to worry about? And how does tragedy and death "sustain" life? How does pain and suffering "advance the agenda of life," which is to "become more of itself"?

These are fair questions, yet they cannot be answered with but a shallow look at what is going on or a glance at the "appearance of things."

In this, as in all things, we must "judge not by appearances."

A matter of perspective

The fact is that everything that happens has a positive outcome; everything that occurs produces ultimate benefit. It may not *appear* that way, but this is because of our limited perspective.

Viewed from the perspective of the Soul (a perspective rooted in Eternity), *nothing* happens that does not move forward the Mission of the Soul and the Agenda of Life (which are the same: to recreate, produce, and experience More of Itself).

I realize that embracing this idea requires an immutable faith in the Process of Life. Yet it is just such immutable faith in Life to which Life Itself calls us. It is this remarkable leap in faith that is meant by *When Everything Changes, Change Everything.* The "everything" we are invited to change is everything we ever thought we knew about Life; everything we ever thought we understood; everything we ever held as "true."

WECCE invites us to throw out the rule book; to start over from scratch; to begin again in our search for eternal truth---as if we had not found that truth before.

When we talk about having faith in the Process of Life, we are talking about faith in God. *Conversations with God* tells us that the words "God" and "Life" are interchangeable. Both words refer to the same thing. Therefore, faith in Life *is* faith in God, and faith in God is faith in Life.

It is easier to have faith in God (if you believe in God at all) when you see the Line of Logic that runs through most of the world's religions and spiritual belief systems.

This logic declares, first, that there *is* a God.

Second, it declares that God is The Creator. God created all things, visible and invisible, and continues to be the power behind all creation to this very day.

Third, this logic declares that God is good. God is Love. God's intentions are benign, and God's wish and desire is to bestow upon us blessings.

Some religions also tell us that God judges and punishes, but even for those religions the first three statements are true. This is the Line of Logic of religions and spiritual belief systems around the world: God exists, God creates, God is good.

True or false?

Now either these things are true or they are not. If they are not true, the discussion is over. There is nothing further to talk about. We live in a random universe, a system with no Supreme Intelligence behind it, no predictable process running it, no purpose or goal or reason for being.

Let's test this theory out. Let's conduct a little experiment...

Experiment #1
"The Eight Week Adventure"

This experiment will take two months to complete. It is predicated on the notion that all of life's "adventures" or "episodes" usually play out in eight weeks or less. True, some of them may take ten or twelve weeks, and some even longer, but most of them, the vast majority of them, move from Start to Finish in eight weeks or less.

We are defining "adventure" here as something that is being worried about. It could be a driving test that is coming up, a court date that's on your calendar, a meeting with the boss, a big date you've been waiting for, the results of a medical exam, or anything else that has had you on edge.

The subject of this experiment, however, is not going to be you. It's going to be someone you know. And so, it's going to require to cooperation of some family members or friends.

Here's what we're going to do...

    1. Ask ten friends or relatives if they would be willing to cooperate with you in a little experiment. When you have ten who have said yes...

    2. Ask each person to list something they are "worried about" right now.

    3. If a person says he or she has not a single worry, find someone else to replace them.

    4. Thank the person for explaining their "worry" and make a note of it a journal or computer file.

    5. Wait two months.

    6. Contact the same ten people whose worries you notated and ask them what is true now about what they were worried about. Keep track of how many people tell you that their worries came true, and how many tell you that what they were worried about never happened.

    7. Of those who say their worries came true, ask how many experienced that outcome as deeply damaging and how many experienced that outcome as actually *beneficial* when all was said and done.

    8. Write an essay about what you feel this experiment has shown you about the validity of "worry."

Now if we *are* part of a conglomeration of atoms and molecules and sub-molecular particles that swirl about in no particular fashion with no particular outcome intended or designed, how is it that the outcomes we noticed in the experiment above produced the results that they produced?

(I already know what results that experiment produces, by the way, because I've done the experiment myself, and received reports from dozens of others who have done so as well.)

Conversations with God assures us that it is *not* true that we live in a universe of random chance. And now, even many scientists are concluding that there is far too much intelligence in evidence everywhere in the design and function of the universe, from the tiniest atom to the biggest chunk of matter out in space, for all of this to be nothing more than a biochemical process of random chance.

Everywhere we look we see evidence of intricate, sophisticated, complex interweavings of every form of life and of every life process, such as to belie the idea that this all came together in this particular way "by accident." The odds are far, far more probable that Life is working as it was intended to, as it was designed to. And here is *how* it was designed to...

The Basic Principles of Life

Life is a self-regulating system. CwG tells us that life is eternally Functional, Adaptable, and Sustainable. In simple terms, it is designed to go on. Forever. And it will do whatever it takes to do that---including die (or what you *call* "die"); including produce disasters (or what you *call* "disasters"). This is true of Life is all its forms---including the form called You.

And that is why there are black holes in space that gobble up star systems. And that is why there are seemingly destructive events---hurricanes, earthquakes, tsunamis, man-made wars, violence---on earth.

> **The mission of the individual soul is to grow in consciousness.**

Life functions effectively to keep Life going and growing, and if that process requires certain changes or events, Life adapts in order to produce those. Life thus renders itself and its process of growth sustainable. How can killing and dying render life sustainable? More lives are saved by some lives being lost than would continue to thrive if those few lives had *not* been lost. Life will unflinchingly alter a part of Itself in order to maintain balance and sustainability in the whole of Itself. A surgeon will amputate a leg without hesitation to save the remainder of the body.

This is what you are now doing. Remember, your purpose in "coming to life" in physical form is to allow God to experience Itself fully and completely, in you, through you, as you. This is the agenda of the Soul---which is God, *individuated*. The Individual Parts of God do whatever is needed in order for the Whole of God to experience Itself completely.

Life is God experiencing and sustaining Itself through the process of Life Itself.

Your mission: soul growth

In order for the Soul to experience being all of that which Divinity is, it must expand to become able to express that. Yet it is not growing in size, it is growing in *consciousness*. The Soul has no "size." It is limitless.

The Soul is the individuated consciousness of God. It is a Part of God which is conscious of Itself to a lesser degree than The Whole. It is the Same Stuff as God (which is Pure Self-Consciousness), but in smaller amount---even as a drop of the ocean is the same stuff as the ocean itself, yet in smaller amount.

The mission of the individual Soul, then, is to grow in consciousness, expanding to duplicate the consciousness of God.

But wait. How can all souls become identical in consciousness to the Totality? Wouldn't that mean there would eventually be as many Totalities as there now are individuated Parts? No. Because the *process* by which the soul's consciousness becomes identical to Totality Consciousness is by the consciousness of all souls expanding to an awareness that there is only One Soul.

The drops of water that make up the ocean do not expand to a point where they eventually become a billion huge oceans. Rather, the drops become aware that they were never separate from the ocean at all! They come to know that the drops *are* the ocean.

This Knowing and Experiencing that we *are* The One is the ultimate goal of each Individual Soul and the purpose of Life---which is to say, the purpose of God. This Knowing and Experiencing happens inevitably and automatically at the moment that we call "death", but it can also happen during our physical lifetime upon the earth. We refer to such moments of Knowing and Experiencing by many names: transcendence, transformation, elevated consciousness, nirvana, bliss, oneness, Samadhi, etc. It is when we merge with The All---yet we don't *actually* merge with The All, we simply become aware that we were never *unmerged*. Our individuated consciousness melts into Cosmic Consciousness and the two become One.

The reason for your experiences

All the experiences of your life are designed to serve this single goal of the Soul. Every event has been and will be aimed at raising your consciousness, or, as some have put it, *waking you up.* All the occurrences of your entire life have fit perfectly into the pattern of soul growth (expansion of consciousness) that is an intrinsic part of your mission here on earth.

Yet why was our consciousness contracted in the first place?, you might ask. Why didn't God just let us Know of our Oneness with Everything, including Divinity, when we were individuated? Why couldn't we have remembered that? Why did we have to forget?

Those are fair questions. They are answered in the CwG books. Do you remember the answers?

> ### QUIK QUIZ
> **What is the purpose of Forgetfulness in the experience of the Soul?**
> **Why do we not constantly know the bliss of Oneness with God?**
> **Write your answers below. Use a separate sheet of paper if needed.**
>
> _____
> _____
> _____
> _____
> _____
> _____
> _____

I hope you know those answers. They are foundational and critical to your understanding of the *Conversations with God* material and the WECCE Technology---which, in turn, can change your whole life, making it a joyous experience filled with Wonder. That is, it will be *wonder full.* As it was meant to be. (If you do *not* know the answers to the questions above, please re-read CwG!)

All of your life experiences are meant to lead you to the wonderful remembrance of Who You Are through the *demonstration* of that in relative terms.

How do I know this about your experiences? *Because you are having them.* You would not be having them if they were not serving this purpose; if they were not, therefore, for your highest good. *Evolution demands it.*

Evolution serves the process of evolution itself. It *must*, or evolution would end. Everything in Life serves the process of Life Itself. It *must*, or Life would end.

CwG tells us that *God is a process.* God is not a Super Being, living somewhere up in the sky. God is the process of Life Itself. And THAT is how we know that we have nothing to worry about.

The 'secret identity' of God

This does not mean that God does not have a personality. Or desires. God does. But if you want things to never change, if you want things as they are right now to never end, this idea of God as a *Process with Personality* will not appeal to you at all. You will want just the opposite to be true. You will want God to be something that is unmovable, unshakeable, static, without change. You will want God to be "as it was in the beginning, is now, and ever shall be..."

Yet God *is Change.* You might say this is God's "secret identity." And all change is change for the better. It can be no other way, because evolution demands it. All of this is a long way of saying that God's intentions---for you and for Life Itself---are that only blessings will be made manifest. Or, to put this another way: Nothing "bad" happens to God...and God is Who You Are.

I have offered this deep discussion here so that you may know the theoretical basis for the statement: *Only Good can happen to me.*

That is a powerful affirmation. As is this: *Nothing exists but Perfection.*

Yet since you don't know *how* perfection is going to present itself, fascination and intrigue can remain. Yet "I worry about how it will all turn out" can change to "I wonder about how it will all turn out" when we know the agenda of the Soul. That is why I explained this in all of the above. Yet how can you know the agenda of the Soul in any given circumstance? How can you relate an individual event in your life to this overall mission of the Soul? By getting in touch with the Soul Itself and meditating deeply, or praying earnestly, or using the **SouLogic** process that I use myself.

Here we go with that process again

Let's take another look at how this can work.

Supposing what has happened is that you have been given a diagnosis of a very serious disease. Now how in the world can *that* be "perfect"?, you might ask. How in the world do you not "worry" about that?

Indeed, it is life's most difficult moments that test all the theories presented here. Yet now we have **SouLogic** to use as a tool to help us understand. We have a pathway from the Mind (which definitely does *not* understand) to the Soul (which abides in a peace that *passeth* all understanding).

If I were able to use the **SouLogic** process with someone who had undergone the experience described above, here is how I imagine that our dialogue might go...

NEALE: Tell me, on a scale of one to ten, how worried are you about this condition that you have been diagnosed as having?

JANICE: A nine or a ten.

NEALE: Thank you, I got that. Now let me ask you another question. Do you believe in God?

JANICE: Yes, I do.

NEALE: Do you believe in the existence of the human Soul?

JANICE: I think so, yes.

NEALE: Do you believe that the Soul is eternal and can never die?

JANICE: I want to believe that, for sure. Especially now.

NEALE: Okay. What do you believe is the relationship between the Soul and God?

JANICE: That's a tough question. I'm not sure I know the exact answer to that.

NEALE: I got that. But if you thought you *were* sure, what would your answer be?

JANICE: I don't know.

NEALE: I know you don't know, but if you thought you *did* know, what would you say?

JANICE: Honestly, I really don't know.

NEALE: Fair enough. You don't know, and you know that you don't know. That's okay. But now let me ask you this. If you could *make up* an answer...any answer that you wish...*then* what would you say?

JANICE: I'm not sure what you're asking me.

NEALE: I'm asking you to invent an answer. Make something up. Everyone can do that. You might not be able to tell me what you "don't know," but you can certainly tell me something that you are making up. So go ahead, use your imagination. Make something up. What is the relationship between the Soul and God? Make up an answer.

JANICE: Uh...the Soul has been created by God.

NEALE: Good. Out of what...?

JANICE: I'm sorry?

NEALE: What is the Soul made out of?

JANICE: Energy. I guess I would say, "Energy."

NEALE: What kind of energy?

JANICE: Is there more than one kind?

NEALE: I don't know. You're making this up.

JANICE; Okay, then I say there is only one kind.

NEALE: Does that mean that God is made up of the same kind?

JANICE: Yes, I suppose so.

NEALE: You suppose so? You're making this all up! In your "made-up" answer, is the energy of God the same as the energy of the Soul?

JANICE: Okay, yes. All of *life* is the same energy, but probably in different amounts.

NEALE: I got it. Good. I see how you are imagining this. So in your imagination the relationship of the Soul and God is that the Soul and God are made up of the Same Thing.

JANICE: Yes, I guess you could say that.

NEALE: No, this is not me saying that, this is you saying that.

JANICE: Yes, but I don't know if this is true. I am just making this up. You're asking me to make something up, and this is what I'm pretending is true.

NEALE: Good, that's exactly what I'm asking you to do. Now, do you imagine that the soul ever does anything against its will, something that it doesn't want to do? Or that the Soul can be victimized or damaged in any way?

JANICE: In reality, or in my 'made up' story?

NEALE: In your 'made-up' story.

JANICE: No. If the Soul and God are the same stuff, the Soul never does anything against its will, and cannot be damaged or victimized in any way, any more than God can.

NEALE: I see. Then what do you imagine, in your made up story, is the purpose of your soul having experienced what it has experienced here? Namely, the sudden diagnosis of this serious disease?

JANICE: (*About to cry*) I don't know. *I don't know.*

NEALE: I understand that.

JANICE: Don't say it. I know…"But if I *did* know, what would my answer be?"

NEALE: Well, we've already established that you don't know, so make something up.

JANICE: Here we go, making stuff up again. Okay…if I was making it all up, I'd say that I have just experienced this so that I can overcome it, so that I can know how powerful I am, even in the face of this.

NEALE: I see.

JANICE: And so that (*her voice is getting stronger now*)…so that I can one day help others with this same disease, so that they, too, can conquer it.

NEALE: I see.

JANICE: (*She takes a deep breath*) Do you really suppose I've been given this to show me that?

NEALE: What do *you* think?

JANICE: (*After a pause*) I think life brings us events such as these so that we can find a new strength within us, and pass that strength on to others as well. And I think that, at some level, it doesn't even matter if I *die* from this, all that matters is *how* I die. Will I leave here feeling sorry for myself, and making everyone around me sad? Or will I move through this, one way or the other, with a smile on my face, so that others around me can be uplifted, and even *gifted* by my having this disease---in which case my whole life, and this part of my life, will have at least produced some lasting good, some enormous benefit, not just for me, but for others.

NEALE: You made all of that up?

JANICE: (*Smiling now*) Yeah. Yeah, I just made that all up. Do you suppose it could be true?

NEALE: I don't know.

JANICE: (*Laughing*) But if you did know, *what would your answer be?*

NEALE: (Chuckling with her) Yes. My answer would be yes, it's true. There's no place else from which you could have gotten such an idea except the Place of All Truth that resides within you; from your Soul. I think your Soul knows what your Mind can barely comprehend.

(*There is a moment of silence. Then…*)

JANICE: I feel better now.

NEALE: Are you making that up?

JANICE: Yes. I'm making up that I am feeling better. I guess I'm making it *all* up. My whole life.

NEALE: You are, indeed. It's good of you to know that. You are creating your own reality, every day of your life; every moment. You can believe whatever you wish.

You can believe what you just said about this condition that you have, or you can believe that it is a terrible tragedy, that something 'wrong' happened here.

You can have it injure you and re-injure you and re-injure you every time you think about it. Or you can heal yourself by knowing that there will be a perfect resolution to this perfect situation, all in perfect time. Healing yourself, by the way, does not mean changing your condition. It means changing the way you *experience* your condition. Is it 'good' or is it 'bad'? Is it 'okay' with you, or is it 'not okay'? You don't have to live in constant worry over this. You can live in love with all of life just as it is now showing up, because you have faith in God and Life that the process---however it turns out---is perfect.

JANICE: I choose that!

NEALE: Good! For it is more than one Master who has said, "As you believe, so will it be done unto you."

So now, on a scale of one to ten, how worried are you about this condition that you have?

JANICE: Well, not nearly as much. I'm just wondering now how it is all going to turn out. In a sense, I see the 'wonder' of it.

NEALE: Great. So thank you for taking part in this process.

JANICE: No, thank *you*.

And that is how these processes often go in our spiritual renewal retreats. I made up that dialogue based on past experience, but that exchange could have been lifted right off of one of our recordings of those events.

But what if...?

Yet what if knowing the agenda of the Soul, what if believing all the positive things you want to believe, does nothing to alleviate your worrying?

That can happen to even the most positive of thinkers. Even spiritual masters sometimes fall prey to the Illusion. Was there not a crying out in the Garden of Gethsemane: "Father, Father, why hast Thou forsaken me?"

I am so glad that story is in the Bible. It has given me great comfort through the years to know that even Jesus---knowing all that he knew, being all that he was---still had his own moments of doubt, his own time of anguished questioning.

I have those moments all the time. Yes, yes, even with all that I have been told and imagine myself to know and share with others, I have those moments, too. We all do. Unless we don't.

So how do we deal with them?

I know how I do. I use another process, an exercise that is also from our spiritual renewal retreats.

Suppose you're worried about not being able to pay your bills, or losing your relationship. Or suppose you've been really impacted by the downturn in the economy and think you could even lose your home. How do you not worry about such things?

Well, you, too, might want to try this little process. It's very helpful, because it places everything into a new context. It's called: *What Would Happen Then?*

- - - - - - ASSIGNMENT #1 - - - - -

Please learn the following process and then run the process on yourself, using a family member or a friend to take the role of Facilitator.

This process is called *So What?*— or *What Would Happen Then?* In my retreats I use both names interchangeably, depending upon the vibe in the room. If the nuance of the moment is highly sensitive, with tears flowing or feelings running high, I use the gentler *What Would Happen Then* to introduce this process. If the nuance is lighter, perhaps a bit frustrating but with not nearly as much open wound, I'll call the process *So What?*

Again, while this is a workshop process, you can use this process with yourself, with the help of a friend who is willing to play the "Facilitator."

This is a one-on-one interaction that is used in situations where a person has announced that he or she is worried or apprehensive about something. When that comes up, I'll often say, "Well, what is it that you are worried about?" And they tell me. Then I'll ask them, "May I do a process with you that might allow you to get down to the bottom of your worries?" In most cases they will say yes.

If you are moving through this process with a friend facilitating you, make sure that you give them permission to be just a little bit tough with you if they need to be in order to help you. Otherwise they may be reluctant to run the process with you, because at some level it may seem a bit cavalier. If they agree to help you, show them this narrative about the process, so that they can know how it works.

When I run through the process with someone I tell them, "In this process I am going to ask you a question that may feel a bit confrontive. May I have permission ahead of time to ask you a confrontive question?" Most people will give you that permission.

Then I'll go on, saying, **"Tell me again what you are worried about."** They will tell me. And I'll say, **"So what? What would happen then? If that happened, then what would happen?"**

And I keep asking that same question. **"What are you worried would happen then?"** And then they will tell me. And then I say, **"Great, I got it. And if *that* happens, so what? What would happen then? What are you worried would happen *then*?"** and keep this round of questions going no matter what they answer, until they get to the bottom on it. That is, until they get to the root worry, the Big Worry, the worry that is behind all the other worries.

At certain times during this process they will say, **"I don't know"**. And that's when you use the **"I Don't Know"** process: Say, **"I know you don't know, but if you thought you did, what would your answer be?"**

They will always have answer. If someone is working this process with you, I promise you, you will always have an answer. But you must press past the limitations of the Mind in order to see it, in order to find it. Okay, so let's take a look at how the process might go, with your friend as the facilitator:

YOUR FRIEND: I'm going to run a process with you now called What Would Happen Then? This is a process designed to help you get to the bottom of what you are worried about, and to see something important about all that.

YOU: Okay, great.

YOUR FRIEND: Well, you may not think it's so great when we get into it, because I may have to get just a little 'tough' with you here. I mean, the process involves my asking a series of questions, and I'm going to need your permission to continue asking those questions, even though it may get a bit aggravating somewhere along the way. May I have your permission?

YOU: Yes.

YOUR FRIEND: Great. So then let me ask you: What is it that you are worried about?

YOU: I am worried that I could lose my job. They're talking about down-sizing.

YOUR FRIEND: So What? What would happen if you *did* lose your job? If that occurred, then what would happen?

YOU: I wouldn't have any income, and I might not be able to find another job that paid as much---or maybe not be able to find a job at all.

YOUR FRIEND: I got that, thanks. But so what? What would happen if you *couldn't* find another job that paid as much, or any other job at all? What would happen then?

YOU: I wouldn't know where I would live. I'm worried that I could have to live with relatives---or maybe even have to live on the street or something.

YOUR FRIEND: I see. And if *that* happens, so what? What would happen then? What are you worried would happen *then*?

YOU: Well, for one thing, I'd be terribly embarrassed and ashamed.

YOUR FRIEND: I understand. And what would happen if you were terribly embarrassed and ashamed. I mean, *so what?* What would happen *then*?

YOU: Well, that's not the real issue. I can handle a little embarrassment. But I might not be able to survive. *That's* the issue.

YOUR FRIEND: Okay, I see the real problem. So tell me, what do you think would happen if you could not survive? What would happen then?

(Ultimately you will get to a place where you see that what you are worried about is that you may die. You will see that all worry is ultimately a worry about death. At this point your facilitator/friend should say: "What would happen if you DID die?")

YOU: I don't know. I don't know what, if anything, happens after we die.
YOUR FRIEND: Yeah, but if you did know, what would your answer be?
YOU: I'd like to think that I'd go on, that I'd continue to exist in another form, and get away from all this.

And that's your friend's cue to say, **"Then what's the problem?"** And you'll start chuckling. You may actually start laughing as you 'get' that there is really no problem.

Or, you might answer the question another way….
 YOU: After I die I may have to come back and do it all over again.
YOUR FRIEND: So what? What would happen then?
YOU: Well, then, hopefully, I'd finally get it right!
 YOUR FRIEND: **Then what's the problem?**

The process, led to its logical conclusion, can only produce a happy resolution. At the end of the whole process there's no such thing as an unhappy resolution—*because life always works out, one way or the other.* There may be some steps along the way, but everything always works out. What makes this apparent to the participant is when the facilitator recognizes the very first positive response to his or her questions and immediately asks, *"Then what's the problem?"*

For instance, you might give a totally different answer, a third answer, to the above questions. You might say: "Then I'd have to put the whole family in a homeless shelter."
YOUR FRIEND: Good. What would happen then?
YOU: Well, ultimately, I suppose, we'd get out. I mean, I'd find *some* kind of job, if it was only street cleaning or doing dishes in the back of some hash house.
YOUR FRIEND: Okay, so what's the problem?
YOU: The problem is, *I don't want to have to go through all that!*
YOUR FRIEND: I got that. But what would happen if you did have to go through all that?
YOU: Geez, *stop it.* I get the *point* already!
YOUR FRIEND: Do you? *Do you really?*

- - - - - - - - - - - - **END OF ASSIGNMENT #1** - - - - - - - - - - - -

The point of this Assignment was to show you that if you are not worried about the ultimate outcome, if you are not worried about what will *finally* happen (even if you think you are going to die and "go to heaven"---perhaps *especially* so), there is no need to be worried about what's happening *now*---or about any of the intervening steps.

And here's the incredible part: This *lack of worry* will *change your whole attitude* and *affect your whole experience.* All the energies surrounding these events will be changed---and that can *change the events themselves.* It turns out that positive thinking *does* have an effect on life events.

If you know you are going to get to your destination and that you can't miss, then you can take any road and you won't be worried or feel stressed for any reason. It's like knowing the end of the movie ahead of time. It's pretty hard to be scared by a suspense film if you know that it ends well---which we all DO know about Life (unless we don't).

I try to see my life as I would see a movie that I know is going to end well. I watch it and I enjoy the creation. And then, I seek to create it anew, to write a new script and play out a new scene each day. But I know that no matter how it looks right now, it will always have a happy ending. Even if I die, it will have a happy ending, because I know that when I die I am going to be Home with God in a Life That Never Ends (which just happens to be the title of a book I have written that you may very much want to read!).

Always remember: Worry is an announcement that something could go wrong.

Instead of worrying, simply allow yourself to wonder. "Gee, I wonder what *this* happy ending is going to be..."

And give yourself permission to notice this: Almost everything that you were worried about "yesterday" never happened. And of the things that *did* happen, almost all of them produced something better, ultimately, than what "was" before.

(Actually, they *all* did, but you still might not be able to see that. There will come a time, however, when you will. There will come a time when you realize that every outcome was the perfect outcome...because there you will be, having experienced exactly what you needed to experience (read that, "chose" to experience) in order to know and create, at the next level, Who You Really Are.

And so we say, *Thank you, God.*

And so, now, to our third promise. Using the WECCE Technology, you can change Expectation into Anticipation.

Nothing ruins relationships (or anything!) faster than expectation. The moment that you *expect* something from anyone you take their freedom away. And freedom is the very essence of Love. So if you truly love someone you will always, *always* invite them to do what they choose.

If you have constructed "expectations" around people and how they are going to behave with you, you are lining yourself up for Big Trouble---and probably, Big Sadness. The same is true if you start lining up expectations about events, and how they should go.

Nearly every expectation---especially if it involves another person---will begin very soon to take on the characteristics of a demand.

When I was a child and my father told me on a summer day to cut the grass, he would always add as he left for work: "I expect it to be done when I get home."

This was a demand, I don't care how you slice it. This was a demand and a command, and if I didn't get it done I received a reprimand.

Command-demand-reprimand...that's pretty much how most of the human race perceives *God.* And since most of the human race understands this God who loves us so much to have lots of demands, it seems perfectly reasonable for *us* to place demands on those whom *we* love so much.

------ ASSIGNMENT #2 -----

This Assignment, like the last one, involves other people. Please do the work, because I believe it will bring you some richer understanding of many of the points being made in this Workbook, as well as in the *Conversations with God* books and in *When Everything Changes, Change Everything.*

What I'm going to ask you to do is call or talk in person with ten people---they can be anybody, family, friends, total strangers at the shopping center---and ask them the following questions, making note of their answers.

(Hint: Never take notes in front of a person while doing "man-on-the-street" surveys. People very often "clam up" when they see a pad and pen come out. Listen very carefully to what they have to say, then, when they are away from you, take out your small, shirt pocket spiral notebook and make a quick entry about what they said.)

PART ONE: The Survey
1. **Where you taught about God as a child?**
2. **According to your understandings as a child, does God command anything? If so, what?**

3. According to your understandings as a child, does God demand anything? If so, what?

4. According to your understandings as a child, does God reprimand us for anything? If so, how?

5. Have your ideas about any of this changed since your childhood? If so, how?

PART TWO: The Results

Please quantify by percentage points the results below.

1. Percent of respondents who said that they were taught about God as a child:

2. Percent of respondents who said that "God commands":

3. Percent of respondents who said that "God demands":

4. Percent of respondents who said that "God reprimands":

5. Percent of respondents who said they don't know:

6. Percent of respondents who said that their views on this have changed:

= =

Again, please actually take this survey. In fact, you may find it interesting to take this survey once a week, or once a month, in a different location, over the course of a year to see what, if anything, changes from time to time or place to place. Oh, and by the way, when you get the survey results, *pass them on to me.* I want to compile these results from many people in many different places. So send them to

Neale@NealeDonaldWalsch.com
Please put "Survey Results" in the subject line

I think it's important that you know what people are thinking and saying about this right now, today, in contemporary times. We are talking here about changing Expectation into Anticipation, and the expectations that people believe that God has of *them* are the same expectations that people then believe it is okay for *them* to place on *others.*

Yet CwG tells us that if God had only one message that She could bring to the world it would be this: "You've got me all wrong."

God commands nothing, demands nothing, and reprimands no one.

There is a very good reason for this. God needs nothing. How could God need anything unless there was something that God is *not*? Yet there *is* nothing that God is not. God is everything in existence---including things material and nonmaterial, physical and non-physical. Therefore everything God could possibly want God *already has*---by virtue of *Being It.*

This is also true of you. The only difference between you and God is that God knows this and you may not.

Unless you do.

When you understand Who You Really Are (an aspect of Divinity, a singularization of The Singularity) you, too, will never command or demand anything. All expectations will disappear.

You've "got it coming"

The whole concept of "expectation" emerges from a larger idea that somehow, someone owes you something. Maybe you think it's your parents who owe you something. Maybe it's your children. Maybe it's your spouse or partner. Maybe it's your best friend or your employer. Maybe it's your country or your government. But *somebody* darn well owes you *something*, and you're going to *get it*...or know the reason why not.

This idea, in turn, is born out of a false thought that there is something you *need*. If you didn't need anything, it would not matter to you *what* was "owed" to you. You would quite naturally just "write it off." Well, the good news is that you don't need anything. *Communion with God* tells us that Need is the First Illusion of Humans. There are Ten Illusions in all, and Need is at the top of the list. It is the initial False Idea. It is "original sin."

It's quite understandable that we humans embraced this faulty notion. The reasons are clear--- and are clearly explained in *Communion with God*, so I will not go into them here. (You will want to read, or re-read, the entire CwG Cosmology, all nine books, if you wish to bring complete understanding to your encounter with this material. This will immeasurably enhance your ability to utilize the WECCE Technology...which, in turn, can change your life!)

Yet the fact that it is understandable that we *feel* there are things we "need" does not make the need itself any more real. Need is *not* real. It is imagined. And the moment we "get" that, the moment we truly understand it, everything in our life will change---including the feeling that somebody "owes" you something.

------ ASSIGNMENT #3 -----

Take out a sheet of paper and write out your answers to the following questions.

1. In what way, if at all, would your life change if you thought that the following statement was true: *Nobody owes me anything*...?

2. In what way, if at all, would your life change if you thought that the following statement was true: *I don't owe anybody anything at all*...?

How others have answered

I have asked these questions in the Spiritual Renewal Retreats that I facilitate. Here is how others have answered...

Question 1:

"It would color the way I feel about certain people tremendously."

"I would lose my resentment of my parents."

"My sense of disappointment in others would disappear."

"I'm sure I would 'lighten up' a lot! I would just let it go, let everything go, and move forward with my own life, free of my anxiety about 'getting back' what I think I'm supposed to 'get back'."

"I would stop worrying about 'what I have coming' from my children."

Question 2:

"Oh, my God...*freedom!*"

"I could do what I want on Sunday afternoon for the first time since my Mom went into the nursing home."

"It would feel as if a tremendous burden had been lifted."

"I'd feel guilty."

"I'd strike out on my own!"

"My whole world would open up before me. I'd be free."

A single word that says it all

There is one word that, through the years, has always come up in my spiritual renewal work with people. That word is *freedom*. It is what all people want, and it is what most people never, ever experience. Not true freedom. Not real freedom.

True freedom, real freedom, means freedom from fear, freedom from worry, freedom from obligations, freedom from burdens, freedom from money concerns, freedom from relationship worries, and, ultimately, freedom from the inner struggle to find and understand and know and fully express the True Self, through a deeper relationship with God.

God *is* Freedom. That is another word for God.

Now wait a minute, you might say. *I thought you said that God is 'change'!"*

I did. I also said that the words *God* and *Life* are interchangeable. All three statements are true. *Conversations with God* tells us that there are several words for God, because God is so huge, so indescribable and non-definable that it is impossible to find one word in human language that captures the Essence of what God is. Yet if we are allowed to use several words we can begin to come close.

God is: One, Life, Love, Freedom, Change, Joy, Peace, Completion, Being. All these words define God. Yet not separately. You've got to lump them together to come up with anything close. Separately they are limiting. Only smushed together and thought of as OneThing can we start to grasp, start to even get a tiny beginning sense of what this Essence called God really is. So we say that God is...

ONENESSLIFELOVEFREEDOMCHANGEJOYPEACECOMPLETIONBEING

Freedom is part of this Essence. And not a small part. For God is the expression of Freedom at its outermost. Nothing controls God, nothing constricts God, nothing hampers God or frightens God or reins God in. God is Life Expressed Without Boundary-Without Limit-Without End.

Put simply, God can do whatever God wants to do. God can have whatever God wants to have. In fact, God *is* everything God could possibly want to have; therefore it is not even a question of God "having" anything in particular, but, rather, of God choosing to *experience* the "havingness" of it at any particular "moment."

I put the word "moment" in quotes there because there is no such *thing* as a "moment." There is only One Moment, and that moment is *Now*. And there is only One Thing, and that thing is All. Yet God can look *into* All Now and peer so deeply as to see its many disparate parts.

> **God can do whatever God wants to do**

The dictionary defines "disparate" not as *separate*, but as "fundamentally different or distinct in quality or kind, including markedly dissimilar elements." In other words...*Life*, in all of its many manifest forms. Now let's look at Freedom more closely, so as to understand its nuance.

In your imagination, place yourself in a giant room in which everything you have ever wanted exists. "Freedom", in such an environment, does not mean that you can have anything that you want. You *already* have it. Freedom means that you can reach for, hold in your hand, and experience whichever part of All that you wish to experience Right Here, Right Now.

This is the kind of Freedom God has. It is, in fact, what God IS. And so, we say that "God is Freedom, expressed." Likewise, we say that...

"God is Oneness, expressed."

"God is Life, expressed."

"God is Love, expressed."

"God is Change, expressed."

"God is Joy, expressed."

"God is Peace, expressed."

"God is Completion, expressed."

"God is Being, expressed."

These Other Words for God help us to understand the nature of Deity---and our *own* nature as well. For we *are* That Which God Is. We are made in the Image and Likeness of God. That is not a figure of speech. That is an actual reality.

This fact of our being carries extraordinary implications...not the lease of which impact the experience we are discussing here: changing expectation into anticipation.

An entirely different state of mind

There is a subtle difference between expectation and anticipation. At first it may seem as if there is none. What's the difference between saying "I expect" that something will happen and "I anticipate" that something will happen?

Well, let's look at that...

"Expectation" carries two nuances, as I experience the word. One nuance is the one I described earlier---the feeling of "requirement" or "demand"---as in: "I expect you to be done when I get home," or "I expect you to keep your promise." The second nuance emerges from a thought that there is a slight chance that something could go wrong. When you walk into a room and throw the light switch you "expect" the lights to go on. Yet if you were the electrician who created and *installed* the light in that room, and it was just minutes after you installed it, you would not "expect" the light to go on; you would *know* it was going to go on. And as you are reaching your hand toward the light switch you would not *expect* the light to go on when you flip the switch, you would *anticipate* its going on from an entirely different place of Mind.

In this sense, Anticipation and Expectation are two entirely different things. I realize this is a delicate difference in nuance, but it is there. It is a difference. Small, perhaps, but important.

The nice thing about Anticipation is that if something you anticipate does *not* happen, you may be surprised, but rarely will you be offended or upset. Whereas if something you *expected* does not happen, you may not only be upset, you may actually be angry or resentful.

The WECCE Technology invites you to move to a more direct experience of Who You Are by making the shift from your Mind to your Soul. In this place Expectation becomes a folly

Chapter Four: Change Resistance into Acceptance

From the Soul's point of view, everything is happening perfectly. There is nothing you could possibly want because everything you could want you already have. You merely need to choose to experience it.

You have all the Oneness you could possibly want, you merely need to experience it.

You have all the Life you could possibly want, you merely need to experience it.

You have all the Love you could possibly want, you merely need to experience it.

You have all the Freedom you could possibly want, you merely need to experience it.

You have all the Change you could possibly want, you merely need to experience it.

You have all the Joy you could possibly want, you merely need to experience it.

You have all the Peace you could possibly want, you merely need to experience it.

You have all the Completion you could possibly want, you merely need to experience it.

You have all the Being you could possibly want, you merely need to experience it.

You have all of these things because you *are* all of these things. Yet you may not know this because you may not have experienced this. And the irony is that you cannot experience this until you know this.

Knowing always comes before *Experiencing* in the expression of Life.

This is important to *know!*

Knowing this will allow you to experience this.

The unknowable is unexperienceable. Fortunately, your Soul (as opposed to your Mind) knows everything. Therefore it is capable of *experiencing* everything, through you as you. All you have to do is express it. (That is, push it out, *get it out of you*.)

To experience Oneness, simply express it.

To experience Life, simply express it.

To experience Love, simply express it.

To experience Freedom, simply express it.

To experience Change, simply express it.

To experience Joy, simply express it.

To experience Peace, simply express it.

To experience Completion, simply express it.

To experience Being, simply express it.

The fastest way to express anything is to be at cause in the matter. Do not wait to receive it, *give it.* Do not try to find it, be *the source* of it. Do not provide it for yourself (you already have it), provide it for another. The act of giving it to another will affirm your havingness of it, for you cannot give what you do not have.

Since you already have everything you could possibly want, everything that is happening in life is perfect, *in that it produces the right and perfect conditions for you to experience your havingness of everything you could possibly want.*

That is why Life is behaving the way it is behaving. That is why Life is producing what it is producing. That is why you are bringing to you what you are bringing to you, through the process of Life Itself.

When you come to know Who You Really Are (see Pg 3 of this workbook: the Ninth Change in the WECCE Technology) you become clear that nothing is happening TO you, and that everything is happening THROUGH you. This is what I call the First Jesus Secret. Jesus knew that nothing was happening to him, and that everything was happening to him. This made it impossible for him to think of himself as a victim in any way.

The Second Jesus Secret is that Jesus was not different from us. Some people *think* that he was, but he was not. Some people want to *declare* that he was, but he was not. Some people have built entire religions around the *teaching* that he was, but he was not. That there is a difference between Jesus and us has been *our* teaching. *His* teaching was just the opposite. Said Jesus: *Why are you so amazed? These things and more shall you do also.*

Exercise 3

1. **Try to remember everything that you have ever been told about Jesus Christ.**
2. **Make a list of all the attributes of Christ, as you understand them.**
3. **In another notation, carry over onto a second list all of the attributes of Christ that you think apply to you.**
4. **What, if anything, does this tell you? Make a notation in your WECCE Journal. (If you not have a WECCE Journal, start one now.)**

If you believe that you are not the same as Jesus, in what ways do you see yourself as different?

If, on the other hand, you believe that you and Jesus were both born as Sons and Daughters of God, made of the Same Stuff and coming into the world with the same capacities and capabilities and connections to the Divine, in what ways do you believe that Jesus was the victim of the circumstances in his life? In what ways do you believe that you are or have been the victim of circumstances in your own life?

Conversations with God tells us that there are "no victims and no villains." It adds that everything that is happening TO us is happening THROUGH us. This means that we are creating our own reality. Yet we are not doing so in a vacuum. Rather, the reality we are experiencing is being created collectively by the lot of us. As the book we are studying states, our *experience* of the reality we have co-created is being created by each of us, individually.

If this is true (and it is), then we are led to ask ourselves: Why would anybody put themselves through what I have put myself through?

That is the key question that *When Everything Changes, Change Everything* invites us to address. If we are responsible (at some higher metaphysical level) for all the creations in and around our life, why in the world would we have created what we have created for ourselves? Why would we have put ourselves through what we have put ourselves through?

This is the same question that WECCE invites us to ask about the man called Jesus. **If Jesus was responsible for all the creations in and around his life, why in the world would he have created what he created for himself? Why would he have put himself through what he put himself through?**

What is your answer to these questions?
Please respond below.

Now that you are clear about why Jesus created his life the way he did, what, if anything, does that tell you about your own life?

Over and over again the WECCE text invites us to enlarge and expand our Point of View about things; to alter our perspective and thus, shift our perception. "Perspective," the text tells us, *"is everything."*

When we encounter the events of our day-to-day lives from the data of the Mind, we are limited in our ability to understand *why* things are happening the way they are happening. We are forced to rely on the Mind's database only---and that database, while magnificent (it has been gathering information about Life from the moment out hearts started beating, many months before we were born), contains only a minuscule amount of information about the process through which we are moving.

Remember, *God is a Process.*

Remember, too: *We are God.*

We are God, in the *process of Being and Expressing Who We Are*, and of *Becoming Who We Are Next Going to Be.*

Divinity wishes only to experience Itself---then to recreate Itself anew, in the next grandest version of the greatest vision ever It held about who and what It is.

In short, God is Life, ever expanding. This the Soul knows. This, the Mind can only begin to comprehend. The Mind has no experience of this. The Soul has been experiencing this forever and ever, and even forever more. To put this in a strange way (but in a way that explains everything), the Soul has forever been experiencing Experience. The Mind cannot understand "experiencing Experience." The Mind can only experience. It cannot *experience* Experience. Nor can it experience Itself stepping outside of Its experience to experience Itself experiencing Experience.

Only the Soul can do this. Therefore, to even understand what I am talking about here, you have to abandon the Mind and its data (which it thinks is All There Is to Know About Life) and move to the perspective of the Soul. Then, having found your way there (and by the way, only a moment, merely a nonno-second, in that environment is all it takes to glimpse this perspective), you can carry back to the Mind the Awareness of the Soul, *expanding the Mind's database* to consider possibilities not heretofore considered with regard to the events of one's life.

The Soul does not possess "data." That is the job of the Mind. The Soul possesses Awareness. The difference between Awareness and Data is like the difference between having a sexual orgasm and

> **Expand your data to include the perspective of the Soul and you will have found the Pathway to Eternal Peace.**

reading about it. I don't care how much you've read about sex and orgasm, when you have a sexual orgasm for the first time it changes your perspective about sex forever, for now you have expanded your database; you know something you could only know through Awareness---an Awareness only obtainable through experiencing Experience.

Remember always, the Mind's experience (from which it creates your reality) is based on *data*. The Soul's experience is based on *awareness*. Therefore, if you want your reality to shift, you must *change your data*. This you can do, by expanding it. Expand your data to include the perspective of the Soul and you will have found the Pathway to Eternal Peace. Enlarge your data to include the perception of the Soul and you will *change everything* about the way you *think about life*. And about any event *in* life.

What will change

The first thing that will change as you consider the events of your life is your understanding of how the things that have happened to you have happened. The second thing that will change is your understanding of *why*. With these two simple changes you will alter your reality forever.

The WECCE technology is about changing your reality. It is not about changing the events of your life, it is about changing the way you *hold* the events of your life. It is about changing your *experience* of those events. And, ultimately, it is about changing your own *future*---by learning how to use your Mind as a *tool of creation* rather than an *instrument of reaction.*

Once you understand that humanity is collectively creating the events of everyday life, and that *you* are creating your own *reality* of those events, you will stop resisting what is happening, because you will realize that it would not be happening unless it was happening for your own good. Why would humanity do something to itself that was bad? Why would Life move in a direction opposite to that which produces its own evolution?

The answer is, it would not. It *can*not.

In short, everything that is happened is happening for your own good. Everything that has *ever* happened has happened as part of your evolutionary process---both as a species, and as an individual within that species.

Yet if this were true (and it is), you could argue that even your resistance of what is happening is for your own good, *so why resist it?* Why bother resisting resistance?

Ah, a wonderful philosophical question! The answer is, there *is* no reason to resist resistance. Resistance will serve you just as wonder-fully as any other human experience. Yet here is a rule of life of which you should be aware: *What you resist persists.*

So it is all a matter of personal preference. It all comes down to what pleases you. Does it bring you joy to see a particular reality persist, or to encounter a particular reality over and over again? If so, go ahead and resist it every time it appears. That will guarantee its *reappearance* throughout your life!

See how powerful the Mind is? See how powerful *you are?*

I tell you, you are creating your own reality...*and you don't even know how you are doing it.*

Yes, but *why* does resistance produce persistence?

Understanding why it is true that *what you resist persists* can be a help here...just in case you do *not* wish a particular reality to keep reappearing all during your life. So let's look at that.

Resistance is a form of energy---and energy is creative. When you resist something, you give it energy. When you fail to resist something, you do not give it energy. You literally starve it of the Energy of Life. The reality then "dies." That is, is ceases to be.

Resisting something places it there. You cannot lean against a wall that is not there. You cannot push back against something that is not there. Therefore the act of pushing back against something *places it there in your reality.* It is as simple as that.

Experiment #2
"The Antedote"

If you keep confronting an unwelcome reality over and over again, there is a way to end the cycle. Here's what we're going to do...

1. In the next week, deliberately create an unwelcome reality. Make it a small one. Nothing terribly significant, just a reality that vexes you. Do something that you *know* will produce this reality. (Examples: Make yourself late for an appointment; deliberately go the "long way" around town, driving into heavy traffic; purposefully dial a wrong number; let your eggs cook too long and eat them anyway, overdone.)
2. Now...*ignore the reality.* That is, allow it to have no effect on you. It will be easy to not let it bother you in the slightest, since you know that *you created it in the first place.*
3. Practice this several times with different small but unwelcome realities.
4. When a larger unwelcome reality "shows up" in your life, apply what you have practiced, causing yourself to notice that *this reality, too, you created in the first place.*

The Divine cure

What I am teaching you with the Experiment above is the Divine Cure. Every doctor knows it. It is an inoculation. It is a "hair of the dog that bit you." It is a little bit of what you want to avoid a lot of.

When you want to avoid the measles, you get a measles shot. Whether you know it or not, *you have just given yourself the measles*. But in a very small dose. A dose that the body's mechanism can work with. Once the body develops this ability, you can be exposed to the measles virus in a very large amount and *not be affected by it.*

Unfortunately, medical science calls this by the wrong name. Medicine says that you are developing a *resistance* to the measles. In fact, you are developing an *acceptance* of it. You have developed the ability to accept the measles virus into your system and have it *do you no harm.*

What most people do not know is that you can inoculate yourself emotionally and psychologically as well as physically. Using the Experiment above, you can practice observing and then experiencing a remarkable truth: You are creating every reality in your life. Using this Experiment, you can "take a pill" and get better when things are going worse. Your medicine bottle is labeled:

ACCEPTANCE

This is the Divine Cure. And it will be easy to take, easy to "swallow", because of what you now know about your reality and the events that are leading you to it. Once you know that the events of your own life are co-created by the lot of us on earth; once you know that nothing can happen to you that is not for your own good, once you know that everything is leading you to your own evolution, once you know that your reality of all events is being created in your own Mind simply by the way that you are thinking about it, resistance drops away. Acceptance becomes a balm. You have found peace at last.

Chapter Five: Change Disappointment into Detachment

This is an easy one. You cannot possibly be disappointed if you are always getting what you want---and you always want what is for your highest good; you always want to evolve. *That is the very reason you have come here.* You are on the earth so that you can know yourself in your own experience, which is *the process* by which you evolve into greater and greater versions of Who You Are. You cannot become a greater *version* of Who You Are until you *know* Who You Are and *experience* that.

I have just explained to you the purpose for all of life. Religion has been trying to tell us this for millennia. "All things happen for a Divine Purpose," religion has been telling us---but it never tells us *what that Purpose is!*

Now you know.

"Mysterious are the ways of the Lord," we have been told.

Not true. There is nothing mysterious about it. You are always getting exactly what you need (read that: *desire*) in order to express and experience the next grandest version of the greatest vision ever you held about who you are version of Who You Really Are.

You are doing this step-by-step, one moment and one condition and one situation and one circumstance and one event at a time. Each moment that passes produces a response from you, and each response produces a Divine Desire for another moment perfectly created to produce the next grandest version of the greatest vision ever you held about who you are.

The response that each moment produces is either a Creation or a Reaction.

If your response is a Reaction, you will literally *reenact* what you did and who you were before. This will set up another moment, another condition, another

> **Most people do not know who they are or what they are doing.**

situation, another circumstance, and another event nearly the same as the first, for the *purpose* of the first event was *not* to get you to *react*, but to *create.*

If your response is a Creation, you will set up a *different* moment, a different condition, a different situation, a different circumstance, and a different event, because you will have *evolved to the next level.*

Again...this is the purpose of all of life.

Repeat after me: *This is the purpose of all of life.*

Our faulty notions

Knowing that you are always getting what is best for you, given your agenda in every moment, makes genuine disappointment impossible. Remember this always: Disappointment (in anything) is your announcement that you do not understand who you are or what you are doing here (on the earth).

Most people are making that announcement daily. Most people do *not* know who they are or what they are doing. This is not an indictment, this is a simple observation. I observe that most people are living a Case of Mistaken Identity and pursuing a Pointless Purpose.

Most people think they are simple little animals on a simple little planet in the middle of a relatively small solar system at the edge of a medium size galaxy somewhere in a massive universe, and that the main purpose of their actions, choices, and decisions is survival.

Nothing could be further from the truth.

You are a divine being, an expression of Divinity Itself. Your survival is therefore guaranteed. You could not "die" if you wanted to. That is the one and only thing that God/Life cannot do.

The closest you can come to it is to Change Form. This you *can* do, and you are doing it all the time. Every moment of your life you are changing your Self. This is true physically as well as meta-physically. The process of cellular reconstitution is ongoing, such that every seven years *all the cells of your body have been replaced.*

You may want to read that again, and closely consider its implication. There is not a single cell in your body that was there seven years ago. So if you woke up this morning "feeling like a new person," it's because *you are.* Like the fabled character in *Star Trek*, you are a Shape Shifter.

However, this does not mean that you are any *different* from the way you were before. "New" does not necessarily mean "different." You could be a "new" version of the "old" you. This would happen if you insisted on recreating yourself anew in the *last* version of Who You Are, rather than in the next grandest version of the greatest vision ever you held about who you are. And *this* happens most often when you are "on Automatic." That is, when you leave the Process of Evolution to "do its thing" by itself, without conscious participation and conscious creation by you.

You see, you are evolving all the time. The question is not whether you are evolving, but whether you are doing so consciously or unconsciously. The choice is always yours.

Barbara Marx Hubbard wrote a wonderful book on this very subject, called *Conscious Evolution.* I commend it to your reading.

Exercise 4

1. **On a sheet of paper write down the names of three people who have been or are now important to you in your life. Leave a big space beneath each name so that you can write stuff in that space.**

2. **Under each name write three ways in which that person has changed through the years, *not counting their physical appearance.***

3. **Next to each change, add your observation about whether you think this change occurred in that person *by design* or *by accident* (that is, without conscious choice or intention).**

4. **If you believe that at least some of the changes that you have seen occur in these people have occurred *by design*, on *purpose*, contact that person and ask them *how they did that.***

5. **Now, on a separate sheet of paper, write down three characteristics or "ways of being" that apply to you as you experience yourself, and that you would like to change.**

6. **Next to each characteristic, write down the date by which that "way of being" will be changed.**

7. **You are engaging in a process of Conscious Evolution. Make a note in your WECCE Journey about how it feels to be doing this thing---and how successful you are at doing it.**

Life invites you every day to notice that you are engaged in a sacred process---what the CwG book *Happier Than God* calls the Process of Personal Creation.

Once you understand this and come to know how the process is working, you will find yourself quite automatically changing Disappointment into Detachment. This will happen without effort. You will be detached because you will know that you cannot be damaged in any way by how things turn out.

Now I know this is difficult to believe. We all want to *define* "damage" in human terms. This is understandable, as these are the only terms we know. And so we quite naturally use these terms as we look at life. We see the earthquake in Haiti and we see that human beings *are,* in fact, damaged. We watch videos of the Asian tsunami and we see that human beings *are,* in fact, damaged. We remember 9/11 and we see that human beings *are,* in fact, damaged.

Yet WECCE invites us to *change everything* about the way we look at life. It encourages us to define life not in human terms, but in spiritual terms; not through the Data of the Mind, but through the Awareness of the Soul.

Is the Soul heartless?

There is a danger here. It is that we may appear heartless. How can anyone look the Haiti disaster in the face and not "get" the damage that has been done? How can anyone call the 200,000 deaths anything but a tragedy? How can anyone define this event as other than a sheer calamity? Yet (to dabble in figures of speech) the Soul is not heartless. It simply sees "disaster" in a different way.

> The real danger is not that we will *appear* heartless, but that we will *be* heartless.

This raises an interesting question" How does God see it? Does God see it as a calamity? Does God see it as a tragedy? If so, why would God allow it---much less *create it?*

These questions lie at the core of every philosophical and theological searching that the Mind of Humans has ever undertaken. We roll our heads on the pillow at night trying to figure this one out. Often, in desperation, we simply disavow God as our means of dealing with what has happened. We say that "no God who is truly a God of Love would ever permit such suffering and death. Therefore, God must be a fiction. *God does not exist."*

The GOD DOES NOT EXIST SCHOOL may leave us reconciled, but it does not leave us satisfied. Nor does it give us *a way to move forward.* It brings us, in fact, to an abrupt standstill; to a throw-up-the-arms disbelief in the randomness of life; to an impotent anger, an empty frustration, an utter disgust with the entire life process---and with our own powerlessness.

This does not bode well for our future, either individually or collectively. We are tempted to get into a groove, fall into a pattern. Our responses will become Reactions, for we will have lost our faith in the power of Conscious Creation. Perhaps even in the *existence* of it.

Do not confuse heartlessness with detachment

The problem of getting into a groove, the real danger, is not that we will *appear* heartless, but that we will *be* heartless; that we will become, out of sheer anxiety about the whole experience, unable to open our hearts to our fellow humans---and ultimately, even to ourselves. This can lead to chronic depression and, in worst case scenarios, place us on a path to paranoia (everyone and everything is against us, including *life itself*), and perhaps even to schizophrenia (the ultimate abandonment of the known self from the known life).

Fortunately, things don't go that far for most people---yet heartlessness alone, without extending into side-effects, is sad enough. And do not confuse "heartlessness" with detachment. They are not the same thing. The person who is detached has simply stepped back from the negative emotional energy surrounding any unwelcome event or circumstance. This allows that person to be *more* effective, not *less*, in responding to it; to be *more* heart-filled, not *less*, in producing a solution.

Disappointment delays solutions, detachment rapidifies them. This is because disappointment is an emotion that has to be dealt with first before the Mind can move forward, whereas detachment is a *State of Mind in itself* which needs no alteration for the Mind to advance in its solution-finding mission.

The Mind can focus on *solution* rather than *resolution*.

This is a huge up-shift. This is a major realignment. This can change everything.

Don't allow yourself to get into a groove

Therefore, don't allow yourself to "groove" a response to certain events or conditions in live. The more you allow yourself to react to the same stimuli in the same way, the more you make it difficult not to. Always remember that the same stimuli are coming at you over and over again for the same reason: not to *close* your heart, but to *open* it. Not to stop your evolutionary progress, but to advance it.

Put in simple terms: There is something that humanity as a whole, and each of us individually, is being invited to remember, understand, and express about Who We Are---and *that* is why the Haiti's and the Katrina's and the tsunami's and the 9/11's keep happening.

The question is not, why is this happening? The question is, what part of ourselves, collectively and separately, are we being invited to step into that will advance our evolution, and...*are we willing to do that?*

Let's move away from huge global disasters for a moment and consider now only the "disasters" and the "bad moments" in our own life.

If we allow ourselves to react in the same way---to "groove a response"---to those bad moments, we will do nothing but recreate them. As I said, grooving our response makes it very difficult to *alter* our response. Our response will continue to be a Reaction and not a Creation...and we have already looked at what *that* produces: more of the same.

One of the most common responses you may wish to avoid "grooving" is that response called "disappointment." Seeing everything as perfect, then peering even more deeply *into* everything in order to find what is there for you to remember (and how you can Create rather than React), will pop you out of the "groove," switch you to a new track, place you on another path---the path for which you have always been searching. As the cover of the book says...

IN A TIME OF TURMOIL, A PATHWAY TO PEACE

Chapter Six: Change Enragement into Engagement

The true master is one who sees *use*, not *abuse*, in the most difficult and challenging of life's events. The master knows that to be *enraged* produces no benefit, but to be *engaged* produces no *end* of benefit. Therefore, the true master is always engaged and never enraged.

The true master engages life in every moment at every level. By "engaging life" I mean she does not walk away from it. He does not head for the hills, run for cover, or lie low until the danger passes.

This gets us back to the first change in that list of Nine Changes That Can Change Everything found on Pg. 3 of this Workbook: Change your decision to "go it alone."

The first thing that most of us want to do when things get tough is to self-isolate. We have been taught to do this; we have been told not to lay our problems at anyone else's feet, etc. Yet self-isolation is the worst thing we can do, because it leaves us alone with our Mind. And the Mind, in a negative state, is not a friend with whom we can safely be alone. It will nag us, confront us with every piece of negatively Judged Past Data that we have stored in our memory bank, and fill us with self-loathing, fear, and apprehension.

SPOTLIGHT ON THE SELF

Take a close look at how YOU behave when something "bad" happens, or when you get sick, or when you suffer a loss (of a relationship, or money, or *anything)*. Do you reach out to *engage* life, or do you become enraged *with* life? Think of three people you could call on right now if you really hit a real downturn---people who would be "there" for you in a non-judgmental way. Make a list of these people and their contact information, then promise yourself to connect with them if things start going bad. Make this an *iron clad* promise.

When you suffer a setback you would be best advised to do exactly the opposite of what you might be tempted to do. Instead of closing down, open up. Instead of hiding out, step in. Instead of slinking away, smile and stay.

The WECCE text says that if you can give yourself this gift, enragement will turn into engagement, and even your anger (a useful tool) can then serve you, allowing you to direct your focus to activities that can alter conditions, rather than simply brood about them.

Conversations with God tells us that anger is one of the Five Natural Emotions. Rage is not. Rage is the emotion we experience if our anger is repressed. The Five Natural Emotions are: Anger, Fear, Grief, Envy, and Love. If these emotions are repressed they turn into very unnatural emotions. Repressed Fear turns into panic, repressed Grief into chronic depression. Repressed Envy turns into jealousy, repressed Love into possessiveness. And repressed Anger turns into rage.

Yet Anger that is expressed can be a gift. It allows us to say "No, thank you." It can be a motivator that pushes us into action. But it should never be the *determiner* of what that action will be. When anger is that which *determines* our actions rather than that which *motivates* them, it's a sure sign that we have become enraged and not engaged. This produces nothing of value.

Getting out of the cage

There is, of course, as escape from all this. Enragement, like disappointment, becomes virtually impossible for you to fall into when you understand Who You Are, and when you *apply that understanding* to your daily life. To do this you will have to bring your Soul's Awareness into your data-bank. Interestingly enough, you can accomplish this through the process of engagement...by engaging in activities that produce spiritual nourishment and open a pathway to the Soul.

Once you are connected to and commune with the Soul---even if only for a nanno-second (as I mentioned before)---the glimpse you will get of EverMoment will expand your Mind's data immeasurably. You will never be able to think of your life in the same way again.

THINGS YOU CAN DO...

- Go to your local Zen Center and spend some time in meditation with others there. If you find Zen meditation takes too much discipline, find another meditation center or group in your area that may be a bit more informal. Nearly all cities and towns have one.
- Seek out a New Thought Church or spiritual center in your community and begin attending not only Sunday services, but enrichment programs offered during the week. (Most churches and spiritual centers offer such programs.)
- Find a local Ecstatic Dance group and give it a try! (You don't have to be a "dancer" to make a real connection with a part of your inner self.)
- Locate a nearby retreat site, and spend some time there.
- Enroll in a personal growth and spiritual development program.

The WECCE text promises that, using the WECCE Technology, you can "change addiction into preference," and you can. The first step in this process is to understand and recognize what an "addiction" even *is*, as we are using the word here.

In my terminology, an addiction is a dependency on something exterior to oneself in order to experience happiness. We can become addicted to many things, including, obviously, several substances, both solid and liquid. But I am not referring to those particular addictions here. I am talking about our addictions to behaviors and outcomes.

You can tell if you are addicted to a behavior or an outcome when the absence of it causes you to lose your happiness. Happiness is not something we actually "lose," in the strictest sense of the word. Happiness is something we abandon. Abandoning happiness is something that you *do*, not something that happens to you. I know that is something which is very hard to believe, very hard to swallow, but it is true. Abandoning happiness is a willful act, not an involuntary response. It may *seem* involuntary, but it is willful; it is something we *do*, not something that happens *to* us.

------ ASSIGNMENT #4 ------

1. Find a copy of *A Handbook to Higher Consciousness* by Ken Keyes, Jr. and read it immediately. You can find it on Amazon.com by pasting this link into your web browser:

http://www.amazon.com/Handbook-Higher-Consciousness-Ken-Keyes/dp/1870845242/ref=sr_1_1?ie=UTF8&s=books&qid=1264993055&sr=1-1

This book was written in the 1970s, but do not let that dissuade you from getting it now and reading it at once. It remains one of the most easy-to-understand and powerful books I have ever come across to help people understand how the Mind can work for you or against you in the creation of your reality.

2. After reading this book, make an entry in your WECCE Journal listing the number of behaviors (in yourself or others) or outcomes (in your life or the life of others) to which you can identify yourself being addicted.

3. Decide which are the Top 3 (in terms of impact in your life) and commit to tackling them one by one, setting a schedule---and notating it in your Journal---as to when you will free yourself from these addictions.

4. Do not fail to do this work. This single Assignment could change your life.

I always tell people who are serious about changing their lives to read Ken Keyes' book. I met Ken personally around 15 years ago, and he was a remarkable human being. He has since celebrated his Continuation Day, but while he was here in his physical body he touched the lives of thousands of people in an extraordinary way.

When Ken would go around the country lecturing, he would always shock his audience when he entered the lecture hall. One of the most positive writers and presenters anyone could ever have found to read or to listen to on tape, Ken stunned his audiences when he appeared live...as he rolled into the room in his mechanized wheelchair and people realized that he was a quadriplegic.

How could anybody be so happy under such conditions?, people gasped. But when he was through with his lecture everyone was very clear. Happiness, Ken told his audiences, was all a State of Mind. It had nothing to do with what was going on outside of you, or what was true in your exterior world. It had everything to do with what was going on *inside* of you, and what was true in your *interior* world.

Of course, *When Everything Changes, Change Everything* makes precisely the same point. The "everything" that it invites you to change is everything that is going on inside of you. Most important, it invites you to change your perspective---which is an interior point of view.

Exercise 5

1. **On a sheet of paper make a list of the last five times you can remember being unhappy. Don't judge yourself about this, just make the list.**
2. **In a second column write down next to each item what, exactly, made you decide to abandon your happiness.**
3. **In a third column make a note of how long you can remember being unhappy about this, and what it was that eventually caused you to return to your happiness.**
4. **Now in a separate section below these columns, answer honestly for each item above if you would be unhappy again were the same thing (or the same kind of thing) to happen to you again. Just write down Yes or No about each of the items.**
5. **For each answer Yes on your survey, ask yourself: What would it take for me to *not* be unhappy should this same thing happen again? Write down your answer.**
6. **For each answer No on your survey, ask yourself: Why would I not be unhappy if this happened again, given that I was unhappy *this* time? What would be different in the future? Write your answer out.**
7. **Keep a copy of this (and every) on-paper Exercise for future reference as you move forward in this Workbook. It can be extremely valuable to look back on these kinds of notations weeks or months from now.**

There is actually nothing in your life that you cannot do without. An "addiction" is nothing more than your Mind telling you that there *is*. There *is* something that you cannot do with
out, and *this is it....*

Then your Mind will "fill in the blank," and because you are basing your understanding on Judged Past Data---information held in the Mind---rather than the Awareness of the Soul, you will believe this to be true.

You can even do without food and water and shelter. Even air. You may, in fact, "die." That is, you may leave your physical body and continue living in another form, in another Realm. But from the perspective of the Soul, this is of no concern. Your life can never end, nor can the process of evolution in which your Soul is engaged, and your Soul does not have a preference as to which Life Form it takes at various points along the way. Only your Mind cares about that---because your Mind is confused about Who You are.

In short, your Soul is not afraid of "dying." And as I observed in the first chapter of this Workbook, when you are not afraid of dying, you are no longer afraid of *living*. Such a frame of Mind makes you, ironically, a very powerful person indeed, someone not likely to "die" of unnatural or unexpected causes---much less lack of food, water, or shelter.

Getting out of the cage

As you move through this Workbook I am sure that you are finding a lot of repetition in here. This is the only way it could be since, in fact, all truths and all solutions and all levels of clarity revolve around the same fundamental information about Who You Are.

I have said over and over again here that most human beings are a living, breathing Case of Mistaken Identity. We don't know Who We Really Are, and holding this piece of information can change our entire lives.

Now you can be *told* Who You Really Are until the cow jumps over the moon and it may not alter anything. Being told Who You Are and *experiencing* Who You Are are two entirely different things. The only way to experience Who You Are is to *express it*. That is, you have to live it, not merely believe it or think it or imagine it or hope it or want it or be told about it. You have to express it...*through* you, *as* you.

> **First you must know Who You Are before you can put that into Life as an expression.**

Yet you cannot express it unless you know it. First you must know Who You Are before you can put that into Life as an expression. And this knowing of Who You Are is not very easily done through the Mind. It is not impossible, but it is very difficult, very challenging, for the reason that we have been giving you all along: the Data of the Mind is very limited. And it has no other data to go on...*unless* it can *enlarge* its database to include information obtainable only from the Soul.

So here we go again, around and around the mulberry bush, circling the same message over and over again. We just said it in the last chapter and we'll say it again: You must include the System of the Soul as *well* as the Mechanics of the Mind in your approach and your process as you move through life if you hope to find any kind of lasting peace, any kind of true happiness, any kind of meaningful understanding.

Viewed from the limited positionality of the Mind it may very *well* seem as if we may never be as happy again as we are now, should we not have a particular person, place, or thing in our life. That is because the Mind's *definition* of "happiness" is very much different from the Soul's. And *that* is because the Mind and the Soul are "up to" different things. Each has a different "assignment." The Mind's job is to help you survive; the Soul's job is to help you evolve. For the Soul, "survival" is not an issue, is it a guarantee. It is not a matter of whether, it is a matter of how. So your Mind and your Soul are "coming from" two entirely different places as they move through the days and times of your life.

You will see how easy it is to move from Addiction or Preference when you use the WECCE Technology on a daily basis. Here is an exercise that may help you. As you do this exercise, seek to answer the questions from your SoulSpace rather than your MindState.

Exercise 6

1. **On a sheet of paper make a list of as many things as you can think of that you, at one point in your life, thought you could never be as happy without as you were with. Be honest with yourself. Go through your life in memory and bring to the front any time that you felt that you just would never be as happy without this person or that job or this particular place in which to live.**

2. **Now notice that you no longer have that, and ask yourself: Do I really think that I will never be totally happy again?**

3. **If your answer is Yes, ask yourself why. Why do you think you will never be as happy as you were before, without this person, place, or thing?**

4. **If your answer is No, ask yourself why. Why do you think it is possible for you to be happy again, as happy as you were before, without this particular person, place, or thing?**

5. **Write your answers out, don't just think them in your head.**

6. **Now take a look at what you have around you right now, today. Look at the people, places, and things that occupy your life. Ask yourself, "What of these things can I never again be happy without?" Write this answer out as well.**

7. **Keep a copy of this (and every) on-paper Exercise for future reference as you move forward in this Workbook. It can be extremely valuable to look back on these kinds of notations weeks or months from now.**

Chapter Eight: Change Requirement into Contentment

The idea that nothing *in particular* is wanted or need in life for you to be truly happy produces a level of freedom that you may never have known before. It allows you to 'let go' of any thought that anything in life is *required*. Not by you, and not any anyone---least of all, God.

Of course, this, again, is the antithesis of everything we have been taught by our religions, by our ancestors, and by our present culture.

As you know from your reading of *Communion with God*, the idea that Requirement Exists is the Fifth Illusion of Humans. This, in turn, grew out of the idea that "insufficiency" exists; that some-how in this Universe of Plenty there is "not enough." There's not enough time, there's not enough love, there's not enough power, there's not enough money, water, oil, or *whatever* it is that we think we need to be truly happy.

If there was enough stuff, there would be nothing you would have to do to get it---whatever it was that you wanted or needed. You would just reach out and it would be there. But that is not how humans decided that it is. They said, *there is not enough.* So now they faced another question: How does one *get* enough? How does one *qualify?* What does one have to *do?*

> **For you to understand all of this you would have to be very familiar with the Ten Illusions of Humans.**

You imagined that there must be something that you had to *do* in order to get the stuff of which there is not enough---something that would allow you to lay claim to it without argument. This is the only way that you could figure out to get everything---including God---divided in your favor without killing and squabbling.

You have to "do what it takes," right? Uh, well...

You imagined this to be The Requirement. You told yourselves that doing this---whatever "it" is---is "what it takes." That idea has held firm to this very day. If anything, it has grown stronger. You believe that when you do the things you need to do, you can be the things you want to be.

If you want to "be happy," if you want to "be secure," if you want to "be loved," then there are things you are going to have to Do. You cannot "be" these things unless you "have enough," and you cannot "have enough" unless you Do What It Takes to *get* enough---to *qualify* for "enoughness."

This is what you believe, and because you believe it, you have elevated Doing to the highest place in your cosmology. Even God says there is something that you have to Do in order to get into Heaven.

This is how you have it put together. This is...The Requirement.

Mind you, now, all of this is based on The Third Illusion---and the Third Illusion is based on the Second, and the Second Illusion is based on the First. So for you to understand all of this you would have to be very familiar with the Ten Illusions of Humans. Are you?

I am aware that many of you who have read *When Everything Changes, Change Everything* may not have read all (or even one) of the 9 books in the *Conversations with God* series. What I would like you to know now is that those books can be pivotal in helping you to understand and change your life.

Everything that appears in the WECCE text is derived from them. The entire WECCE Technology is based on them. As I noted in the Introduction to this Workbook, *When Everything Changes, Change Everything* is a compilation and a condensation of the 9 *Conversations with God* books.

If you have not read those books---or not read all of them---I want you to seriously considering doing so now.

One of the biggest mistakes made by some people who have read the first CwG text, or, perhaps, the entire opening trilogy, is to assume that they've read all there is to read, seen all there is to see, gotten all there is to get, of the *Conversations with God* message.

Wrong.

Each of the CwG books holds new, not-mentioned-before information, designed to move the message forward, so as to present by the end of the 9-book series a complete picture, a *cosmology*.

It is true that there is some repetition of earlier points in the latter books. The Source from which these dialogues came apparently decided that this was necessary in order to make it possible for anyone to enter the conversation mid-way through, to begin their reading after being introduced to one of the later texts, and have some basis for understanding what was being discussed.

Yet this circling back over previously explored material should not be mistaken to mean that there is *nothing new* going to be presented. And so if you have not read *all nine* of the books in the *Conversations with God* series, you have missed a great deal.

The entire cosmology

Some people do not even know that there *are* nine books in the series. So, just for the record, here is a list of all the titles:

Conversations with God-Book 1
Conversations with God-Book 2
Conversations with God-Book 3
Friendship with God
Communion with God
The New Revelations
Tomorrow's God
What God Wants
Home with God in a Life That Never Ends

The books are divided into what is called (a) the Original Trilogy; (b) the Middle Books; (c) the Second Trilogy; (d) the Final Text.

Do not be discouraged...wonderful insight awaits

Now I know that if you have read none, or only a few, of the books above, that list might seem daunting. Yet if you feel that the WECCE material (which I assume you *have* read, or *what are you doing here?*), or the messages in *any* of the CwG books, has brought you benefit, wait until you've absorbed the entire cosmology. It can create in you a deep and rich understanding of how life works, of *why* it works the way it works, and of how you can make it work better *for you.*

For instance, if you have read *Communion with God* you know about the Ten Illusions of Humans. In that book God reminded me that "there's no such thing as the Ten Commandments." But, God said, "even if you thought there were, you're not keeping them anyway. But it's worse than that, because what you *are* living is The Ten Illusions."

The Illusions are ideas that we hold that create the framework of our entire experience as humans. If you've read *Communion with God* you know what these Illusions are, right? Well, let's see...

QUIK QUIZ

What are the Ten Illusions of Humans?
List as many of them below as you can remember:

1. _____
2. _____
3. _____
4. _____
5. _____
6. _____
7. _____
8. _____
9. _____
10. _____

If you were unable to list these Ten Illusions of Humans, you have missed or forgotten one of the most meaningful messages that anyone could ever have given you---and the most important information in the entire *Conversations with God* dialogues.

I urge you, I encourage you, to go without delay to the text of *Communion with God* and learn about these Illusions. I will list them here, but that will not be nearly enough. The text devotes one chapter to each of them, explaining them in detail and describing how to use them as tools in the creation of the life you deserve and desire.

Here are the Ten Illusions of Humans:

1. Need Exists
2. Failure Exists
3. Disunity Exists
4. Insufficiency Exists
5. Requirement Exists
6. Judgment Exists
7. Condemnation Exists
8. Conditionality Exists
9. Superiority Exists
10. Ignorance Exists

Once you understand that *nothing is required of you* by Life in order for you to justify taking up space upon the earth, you will, in turn, *stop requiring anything of Life* in repayment for It having placed you here! You will stop requiring anything of God, as well. And when you do *that*, you will have graduated. You will have learned all of need to learn to create a happy, joyful, peaceful reality.

Then you will have mastered life. You will have turned Requirement into Contentment. And then you will be ready to do the work that you really came here to do, which is to help *others* master life.

Oh, yes, I didn't tell you that yet, did I...? Hmmm...okay, you might as well hear it now as later...

Your life has nothing to do with you.

I know that you *think* that it does, but it doesn't. It has nothing to do with the Singular You that you imagine your Self to be, and it has everything to do with the Plural You that you Really Are. That is, it has to do with The Whole of You, not merely with a Part of The Whole. And yet the wonderful and blessed irony is that when the Part of the Whole stops concerning Itself with that One Part, and begins concentrating on *all the Other Parts*, everything that the One Part could ever seek or desire comes to that One Part automatically.

This is another concept that might be difficult to understand or to embrace as a functioning truth if you have not given yourself permission to read the entire CwG cosmology. So, again, I urge you to so do. Your entire life will change.

One of the first things that will change---and the most important of the things that will change---is the idea that you are separate from God, separate from Life, and separate from anyone or anything else.

The idea that you are separate stems from the illusion that Disunity Exists. When you thought there was only One of You, you experienced that there was always Enough, and so there was nothing you had to do in order to experience or have anything. The idea that requirement exists cannot be supported inside of the idea of Oneness. Who would require what of whom?

> **There is only One Illusion, the First Illusion: the Illusion of Need.**

And now we see how the dominoes fall, for the idea of Disunity is based on The Second Illusion: that Failure exists. Because God failed to get what He wanted from humans (so the story goes), He separated all humans from Him. So God's failure produced Disunity.

And the idea of Failure was based on The First Illusion: that Need exists. God could not fail to get what God wanted if God wanted nothing, and God would want nothing if God needed nothing. So we see that Need is necessary for Failure to be possible.

In truth, there is only One Illusion, the First Illusion: the Illusion of Need. All the others are permutations of that. Everything else is an expansion of the Only Illusion, with a slightly different nuance.

Yet when you know and fully embrace Who You Really Are, the idea of Need (and with it, the idea of Requirement) is seen for what it is: *an illusion.*

What is contentment?

Contentment is knowing that there is nothing you have to do, nowhere you have to go, and nothing you have to be except exactly what you are being Right Now. Contentment is understanding that you are okay *just the way you are*, and that everything is rolling out perfectly exactly the way it is rolling out; that everything is going according to plan. The "plan" is for you to be able to accept everything that is happening right now as perfectly suited to your Soul's purpose, for your Soul's purpose is to evolve through the knowing and the experiencing of Who You Really Are, and it is using Life (and all its events) as a Tool with which to do that.

"Judgment" is your idea that something that "is" is not supposed to be that way. This ignores the fact that if it wasn't supposed to be that way, it wouldn't be.

I want to repeat an Awareness here that I have placed in the space before, both in the WECCE text itself and in this Workbook: Life is occurring exactly the way evolution induces, in every single moment. Life is always Functional, Adaptable, Sustainable. These are the Three Principles of Life, and they are inviolable. Life could not have been going on for billions and trillions and ka-zillions of years if this were not true. Life adapts *moment-to-moment* in whatever way produces the most benefit to Life Itself. We cannot always see the benefit, therefore we sometimes judge what is happening as being "not okay." We call it that. We label it that. Yet that does not mean that it *is that.*

Often what we label as "not okay" is *very* okay with the Universe. In fact, *always* that is true. It is true because the Universe is incapable of "error." That is to say, *God* is incapable of making a "mistake." How can God make a "mistake" and still be God?

This is the fundamental question that every theology on our planet must address: Is God capable of making a mistake? If yes, and God is not infallible, how can God be "God"? If no, then how can anything that is happening be said to be "not okay"? How could anything be happening "against the Will of God"?

Yet if everything that is happening IS the Will of God...why would God "will" so many horrible things to occur? Or could it be that those things that we *call* "horrible" are not horrible at all? Could it be that, in God's World, it all makes perfect sense?

God the messer-upper

When we judge something, we are calling God 'wrong.' We are telling God that She doesn't know what She is doing. We are saying that He has lost His mind...or at least lost His way. We are claiming that we are Children of a Lesser God. A God that is capable of messing things up, of not getting it right, of failing. Yet even as we pronounce that this thing or that should never have happened, we announce our belief in an infallible God.

We've gotten around this apparent contradiction by saying that nothing happens against God's Will---but that God's Will is simply incomprehensible to Man. *And this is true*, so long as we continue to insist on contemplating daily events using solely the Mechanics of the Mind. Only if we employ the System of the Soul *in collaboration* with the Mechanics of the Mind can we begin to see what God sees, to understand what God understands, and to experience Life as God experiences Life ---wondrously, joyously, endlessly.

The problem around all of this is that many religions have said that things can happen that *are not* God's Will. Further, these religions say, when such things happen, God doesn't like it. God has a *judgment* about it---and a judgment about all those who *took part in it.*

Armed with this teaching about God, we humans have decided that Judgment, as a practice, must be "okay." Having been told that we were made "in the image and likeness of God," we, too, therefore, pass judgment. On each other, and on everything from the weather to the price of tea in China. And we do so with impunity. *After all, isn't this what God does?*

This line of logic is the main reason why humanity *cannot let go of its teaching of a Judgmental God.* Were we to let go of that teaching, we would have to let go of our own self-granted privilege of judging---and we have *no intention of doing that.* For if we let go of judging, we let go of *power.*

Experiment #3
"Judge and Jury"

Beginning this week keep a Judgment Journal. Go to the drugstore and pick up one of those shirtpocket spiral notebooks and carry it with you wherever you go. Or hop over to the electronics place and grab one of those tiny digital memo recorders that they sell and stick it in your pocket or handbag.

1. In the next week, every time you see something that brings up a judgment in you (don't worry, you'll be able to tell), whip out your Judgment Journal and make a note of it. Be honest and say exactly what about that you don't think is "right," or what you don't like, and why.

2. In a second section, write down or dictate a note about where you think that judgment is "coming from." Take a look at what is giving birth to the thought you hold that says that this person, place, or situation should be different. Find out what's *behind* the thought of something's "not okayness."

3. After you have done this for a month, review your Judgment Journal entries and begin to categorize the judgments you have made. For instance, Things People Do That They Shouldn't Do; or…Things People Say That They Might Be Better Off Not Saying, or That They Shouldn't Say….or….Things People Wear That They Don't Look Good In….or whatever.

4. Really keep this journal for a month. Really. It is not a self-indictment, it is simply a little tool to allow you to become aware of what goes on in your Mind, and where it is all coming from. Then, after a month, over the course of the next few days, ask three friends what *they* would think if they encountered one of the people or situations that you encountered that you thought was "not okay." Try to describe what you encountered as objectively as possible, and don't tell your friends how you felt about it, just ask them if they would be willing to share with you what they think their reaction might have been. Tell them you're conducting an experiment and you're taking a survey of people's reactions to certain situations.

5. After they give you *their* reactions, ask your friends to share with you what they think is inside of *them* that gave birth to the ideas they've just shared.

6. In your larger WECCE Journal make a note of any observations you make about yourself and others as a result of these experiences and exchanges.

7.   Now, in the next month, make it a daily practice for you to shift your Judgments to Observations in as many situations and circumstances as possible. Notice when you begin to feel a "judgment" coming up and heighten your awareness of exactly what that feels like. How does it manifest in your body? How does it "feel" in your Mind? Keep watching yourself this way until you can identify the feeling of Judgment almost before it presents itself in fullness. Then, just shift into Observation as quickly as possible. Use this as kind of a Zen practice. It can even be a meditation of sorts. To learn more about the difference between Judgment and Observation read the rest of this Workbook chapter.

What is judgment? What is observation? What is a preference?

Let's define judgment. If you are saying (to yourself or another) that something is not okay, you are in judgment. Saying that something is "not okay" is not the same as saying that something is not your preference. You can have a preference in the matter without making a "judgment" about it.

For instance, in ice cream I have a preference for chocolate. That does not mean that I think vanilla is "bad," or "not okay." I simply prefer chocolate. In colors, I have a preference for blue. That does not mean I think red is "bad" or "not okay." I simply prefer blue.

An observation is a simple statement that says "what' so." A judgment is a statement that says "so what?" When you add the *so what* to *what's so*, you've fallen into judgment.

All of your judgments come from the databank of your Mind. None of them come from your Soul. It is your Mind which is comparing what is right in front of you with what you saw or heard about before. And it is your Mind which is saying that what is right in front of you is "okay" or "not okay," based on this comparison. Your Soul does not hold ideas of "Okay or Not Okay", "Right and Wrong", "Good or Bad". *Everything* is okay in the experience of the Soul. This is because everything is of your own creation. Nothing is being foisted upon you. Nothing *could* be, given Who and What You Are.

Only if you are living a Case of Mistaken Identity could you not know this. Once you drop this false identity, you may not know *why* you are creating a given Reality, but *that* you are creating it will no longer be questioned by you. And with the end of that questioning will come the end of your judging.

> **God judges no one because there is no one to judge, save God. *God is all there is.***

This is exactly the reason that you can believe that God does not judge. Why would God judge Godself for the very thing that God Itself is creating? If God did not like something, God would simply not create it in the first place, right? (Unless we have a *runaway god* who creates things He hates, then blames everyone else for it...)

The only way that the idea of a judging God can be rationalized is if we think there is something in existence that God did not create. So we come up with all sorts of improbable explanations, like "The Devil made me do it!" Or, perhaps, the more conventional theological concept of "free will."

According to this concept, God gives us all Free Will to do as we please. This means that we can actually do something that is against the Will of God. Yet God *allows* us to do this. Therefore, technically, it is *not* against the Will of God.

Sooner or later we have to ask ourselves, *What kind of God is this?* Why kind of God says, "Go ahead, do as you wish! I give you Free Will!". and *then* says: "Ooops, I didn't mean *that!* Now you're going to get it. You're a very *bad person* and I'm going to *punish you!*"

Only a maniacal God, who sets people up to lose and then judges and punishes them for doing so, would or could play a game like that.

Yet this is not how it is. This is not the way things are. There is no such *thing* as Judgment. It is the Sixth Illusion of Humans. God judges no one because there is no one to judge, save God. *God is all there is.* We are all manifestations of the One Thing That Is. We are all Singularizations of The Singularity. We are all Individuations of the Divine.

Now I know that I am repeating myself over and over again here, but this is the single most important message of *Conversations with God* and it cannot be said too often:

ALL THINGS ARE ONE THING. THERE IS ONLY ONE THING, AND ALL THINGS ARE PART OF THE ONE THERE IS.

Even if there were more than One Thing, God would still have no reason to judge us for what is happening or what we are doing, because God knows that everything that is happening is being created *for* us *by* us in order to set up the Right and Perfect circumstance for the Right and Perfect opportunity to make the Right and Perfect Choice as we seek to express and demonstrate Who We Really Are. Everything that is occurring is just such a "set up." Everything we are doing we are doing in response to what we are creating...all of it as part of a larger process called Evolution.

Clear?

Once we understand this, judgment drops by the wayside. Everything that happens, everything that we ourselves do, simply becomes part of the passing parade. We watch it, we observe it, but we don't label it "good" or "bad," "right" or "wrong," "okay" or "not okay." It simply is what it is and it's not what it's not, and that's what true about that.

------ ASSIGNMENT #5 ------

1. Find a copy of *Loving What Is* by Byron Katie and read it immediately. You can find it on Amazon.com by pasting this link into your web browser:

http://www.amazon.com/Loving-What-Four-Questions-Change/dp/1400045371/ref=sr_1_1?ie=UTF8&s=books&qid=1265161470&sr=8-1

This book is one of the most important reads of the past 25 years. When you learn how to do The Work as created and inspired by Katie, you will have passed a milestone in your life. I cannot recommend this material highly enough, and I consider it a "must" assignment in this Workbook.

Chapter Ten: Change Sadness into Happiness

Sadness and unhappiness are not the same thing. Did you know that? Once you know that, you will never be unhappy again. You will have discovered that sadness and happiness are not mutually exclusive.

As you may know, I wrote a book called *Happier Than God.* In that text I wrote that happiness is your natural state of being, and that you can occupy that space all of the time. You never have to be unhappy again. This does not mean that you'll never be sad again, but that, to repeat, sadness and unhappiness are not the same thing.

During the writing of *Happier Than God* my dog, Lady, died. She had been my companion for over 14 years. In the previous 12 months she had become increasingly pain-filled, from a variety of ailments and conditions. Toward the end she was stone deaf and could hardly walk. In the very last days she could not even raise herself up.

I was sad when she died, but I was not unhappy. Can you see the difference? This is *not an unimportant difference.* This is *not a trivial distinction.*

I was sad that Lady was no longer with me, but I was happy that she was no longer in pain. I was happy---very happy---that she had gone on with her journey, celebrating her Continuation Day. I was even "happy that I was sad," because my sadness said something TO me ABOUT me. It said that I cared. It said that I loved. It said that I was human, and that despite the way that the world was showing up around me, desensitizing everyone, I had stayed in touch with my humanity. Yes, I was *happy* about my sadness, and about what it told me about Who I Am. It felt good to be sad.

SPOTLIGHT ON THE SELF

Take a close look at your own experience. Can you think of a time when you were sad without being unhappy? Many a father has felt this as he gave away his daughter in marriage. Many a mother has felt this just after birthing a child. Can you think of such moments in your life? What does this tell you about sadness and happiness?

A key teaching, an important learning

Your sadness does not have to make you unhappy. Used as a marker of where you are on your evolutionary path, your sadness can be a source of inner confirmation of the depth of your feelings, and thus, of who you are as a person and a spiritual being.

Therefore, when someone dies, let yourself grieve. When someone hurts you, allow yourself sadness. And especially when you hurt someone else, allow sadness to accompany your regret. Give yourself the gift of sadness and you will find that you heal more quickly from every experience that would tempt you to forget the fullness of your true identity.

In the months before publication of *Happier Than God*, while I was talking about its contents in speeches, workshops, and public presentations in the media, I began receiving e-mails from people asking about all this. The following, from a woman named Barbara, typifies these inquiries:

Dearest Neale...If we all were happy all the time...IMAGINING...heaven as a place without pain, suffering or judgment...was it God's intention, as He created us, and gave us all our emotions, that we never be sad?

My response to Barbara:

No, Barbara, that was not God's intention. Sadness and unhappiness are not the same thing. A person can be happy being sad. Sadness is a great gift, and widely misunderstood by most human beings, who try to avoid it. I never try to avoid sadness, but rather, move right into it when I am feeling it. Sadness confirms my humanity--- and that confirmation makes me happy.

For instance, what kind of a person would not be sad at the conditions in which most people live on our planet? What kind of a person would not be sad at the death of a loved one, or the loss of a lover, or the news of a friend's misfortune?

Yet these moments of sadness need not interrupt our happiness, but can add to it. For sadness creates a Contextual Field within which our happiness may be more richly and fully experienced.

> **Moments of sadness need not interrupt our happiness, but can add to it. For sadness creates a Contextual Field within which our happiness may be more richly and fully experienced.**

(Parenthetically let me add here something that I wrote not long after the horrific earthquake that struck the island nation of Haiti in the second week of 2010. It is a thought that comes from my friend Gary Zukav. Gary and his beloved, Linda Francis, live just a short distance from my wife Em and me in Ashland, Oregon. About ten days after the earthquake, Gary and I both attended a local fundraiser (a dance with live bands playing all evening) for the Red Cross operation in Haiti, and Gary was asked to say a few words.

Celebrating in the midst of tragedy?

One of the things that Gary said really struck me. It had to do with how one could feel good at a time such as this. Gary put it this way...and I am going to paraphrase here, because I don't remember his exact words, but this was the gist of it:

"How can we come here to this fundraiser and dance and enjoy this music and have fun with each other when there is all that suffering and death and misery in Haiti? This is a question I ask myself when I see the wonderful life I live and the unbelievable challenges faced by others.

"My answer is, the best way to honor those who died in the Haiti earthquakes is to celebrate life. We want to do all that we can to help those who are suffering in Haiti, and I urge you to do that with your contributions here tonight, but we do nothing to honor those who lost their lives through this tragic series of events by wallowing in sadness, with all the good fortune that surrounds us in our owns lives.

"Let us *celebrate* our wonderful good fortune, and give it meaning and value and purpose, even as we share what that good fortune has brought us in the way of personal resources with those who have so much less---and who have had even that taken from them. We can help, and one of the ways we can help is to fully live, and completely embrace, the wonderful life we have been given, with gratefulness for all of it even as we share of its abundance.

"There is no benefit in us feeling ashamed or embarrassed or in some way 'guilty' about all the good that is flowing to us while others are suffering. Rather, we can *use* our good fortune to lessen the bad fortune of others."

I liked those thoughts from Gary, and I thank him for them. I watched Gary experience happiness at the fundraiser that night, even as he experienced sadness about the Haiti events.

What spiritual masters know

All spiritual masters know what Gary said that night at the fundraiser, and what I am saying here. All spiritual masters experience deep sadness. They also experience highest happiness. At the top of this circle, where the two ends meet, is bliss.

Yes, one can be blissfully sad and blissfully happy. For bliss is the experience of the Self, fully expressed and fully experienced.

So the next time you feel sad, experience it full out. Then watch how happy you feel. There's nothing like a good cry, and we all know that the deep, cleansing grief of loss can open you as nothing else. It is sadness that is repressed, rather than expressed, that creates unhappiness, leading to chronic depression. People who seem to be continually sad are not expressing sadness, they are merely talking about it. Sadness fully expressed disappears.

> **There's nothing like a good cry, and we all know that the deep, cleansing grief of loss can open you as nothing else.**

What I am saying here over and over again for emphasis is that your sadness about anything need not stop you from being happy. Happiness is a cumulative thing. If you collect enough of it, it carries you over the moments of sadness in your life. It becomes larger in your experience the more you feel it. I feel happier now than I did in the days before Lady laid down her body for the last time, even though I miss her and I'm sad that she is gone. I feel happier now than when I was 50, happier than when I was 30, happier, in fact, that I have ever been in my life.

And I have learned how to accommodate my sadness and hold it within *my happiness, making it a wonderful part thereof. Indeed, I have learned that without sadness, happiness would be impossible, and that it is achieved through the simple process of embracing all of life exactly as it is.*

We just spoke about this moments ago when I recommended that you closely read Byron Katie's remarkable book, *Loving What is.* The above few paragraphs are a direct lift from *Happier Than God.* That, too, is a book that you could benefit from reading.

------ ASSIGNMENT #6 ------

1. Find a copy of *Happier Than God* by Neale Donald Walsch and please read it, if you have not already done so. You can find it on Amazon.com by pasting this link into your web browser:

http://www.amazon.com/Happier-Than-God-Extraordinary-Experience/dp/1571745769/ref=sr_1_1?ie=UTF8&s=books&qid=1265162182&sr=1-1

This book contains wonderful insights into what is NOT often said about the so-called Law of Attraction that became all the rage when the movie *The Secret* was the Big Hot Thing a couple of years or so ago---including information on the Law of Opposites...which is hardly ever mentioned at all. Most valuable of all: the book's "17 Steps to being happier than God."

> **What you do not hold you cannot heal. So you must hold your experience, embrace it, engage it with loving kindness, bless it, and *then* send it on its way.**

I am going to do something now that I rarely do. I am going to lift another entire section, verbatim, from a previous book.

I am re-printing this here because I want you to know that I am very much aware that simply "holding good thoughts" about our life and our world is not the be-all and the end-all of how to find happiness in the midst of sadness.

There are times when things are really bad, and no amount of positive thinking can change that. Things just are what they are. You can't cover it up, you can't pretend, you can't make it something other than it is. Yet you are not without tools even in this instance.

First, do not resist what is occurring. I said it before, in Chapter 4 of this Workbook, and I'll say it again: *What you resist persists.* So when something really bad happens---this is going to sound strange, but---bless it. Bless all the people and events that are disappointing you, that are besetting you, that are assailing you like so many arrows from afar.

Accept and receive the energy, because only then can you heal it. What you do not hold you cannot heal. Remember that always. What you do not hold, you cannot heal. So you must hold your experience, embrace it, engage it with loving kindness, bless it and *then* send it on its way.

Second, remember that exterior conditions cannot create interior conditions, ever. So, no matter *how* bad things get, the interior of you (your heart and soul and mind) cannot be affected by that which is exterior to you in any way except as you decide that it will.

You are still in charge of your own experience. That is what the WECCE Technology is all about. That is the point of the whole book.

Being in charge of your own experience is not some pie-in-the-sky, totally-out-of-reach ideal, this is something that many people have shown it is possible for all humans to do. The list of those who have endured enormous hardship and great difficulty in their life and still embraced a non-condemning, non-attacking, peaceful attitude is legend, and far too long to print here.

These are normal people, ordinary folks just like you and me. They maintained their equilibrium through physical pain, emotional injury, personal and professional defeat, and more. Nelson Mandela is but one example of what I'm talking about. Christopher Reeve, the actor whose skyrocketing career was brutally interrupted when he was thrown from his mount during a horse show and wound up paralyzed from the neck down, is another. There have been many more. How did they do it?

Somehow they reached back and found the courage within them to keep moving through the events with which they were confronted, to frame them in a new way in their minds, and thus to transform and shape their experience, turning it into something from which they could grow---and actually receive *benefit*.

You can do the same, using the WECCE Technology; shifting from the Mind to the Soul, and using the awareness that you find there to soothe the Mind's jitteriness and quiet its need to do something about what is going on.

My own life experience (I spent a year of my life living outside, in the weather, as a "street person," when I fell through the cracks of the social welfare system and was down to, quite literally, my last nickel) has taught me that the universe is a friendly place. You would think that a year on the street would have taught me exactly the opposite, but I learned even there, through all that turmoil, that God is on my side, and that I am never alone in facing the trials and tribulations of my life.

> **Thank you, God, for helping me to understand that this problem has already been solved for me.**

I learned more. I learned that those trials and tribulation are actually gifts, helping me to remember, to experience, and to express Who I Really Am---which is what I came here to do. I learned that all things happen to serve this purpose. Now I say two prayers that I just love. The first:

Dear God, I thank you today for that which is in my world and in my life. I rest my heart in the knowing that I will yet see pain turn into joy, sorrow into gladness, and even death into everlasting life.

The second: *Thank you, God, for helping me to understand that this problem has already been solved for me.*

This may sound like I am a person who always keeps his cool, and I can assure you I am not. But I do keep my cool more now than I ever did. And I do know that I am on a journey here, a journey having nothing to do, in the end, with my body, and everything to do with my soul. It is a *soul journey* I am on. And so I continue marching Homeward, understanding that every step along the way leads me to my eventual and ultimate and wonderful reunion with God, wherein which peace and joy and love without end resides.

What I am saying here is that you are here for a higher purpose, a grander purpose, than simply getting through life and ending up with the most "toys." You are on a mission of the Soul, to evolve and to become the next grandest version of the greatest vision ever you held about who you are version of Who You Are. This is a joyous mission, not an arduous task, and God is with you, even unto the end of time. And when you experience the ever-present love of God, in you as *you, you will be happier than you have ever been before, and your journey will be wonder-filled.*

How to be happier than God

We see, then, that in the strictest sense we are not talking in this chapter about changing Sadness into Happiness, but about experiencing both simultaneously.

When I coined the phrase "happier than God" I was using the term as the Ultimate Superlative. I remember talking to a friend once about a mutual acquaintance of ours who he described as having "more money than God." I never forget the phrase, because I knew instantly what he meant. He meant, more money than you could possibly imagine. More wealth than even Deity Itself, if such a thing was possible. That's exactly how I use the phrase "happier than God."

I do think it is possible to be happier than you could ever imagine. And I think that the 17 Steps to Being Happier Than God in the HTG text, taken together with the WECCE Technology in *When Everything Changes, Change Everything*, provide us with an amazing set of tools with which to fashion the life of which we have all dreamed---and which is our natural birthright.

THINGS YOU CAN DO...

1. Bring an end to Separation Theology

2. Stay in touch with who you are

3. Give others every experience you seek

4. Be clear that nothing you see is real

5. Decide that you are not your 'story'

6. Have only preferences

7. See the perfection

8. Bypass the drama

9. Understand sadness

10. Stop arguing with life

11. Drop all expectation

12. Have compassion for yourself

13. Speak your truth as soon as you know it

14. Watch the energies, catch the vibe

15. Smile

16. Sing

17. Know what to do when things are really bad

Some of these ideas have already been discussed here. These are the 17 Steps to Being Happier Than God. For full and very clear instructions on how to take each of these steps, see the text of *Happier Than God.* You will be very glad you did.

Chapter Eleven: Change Thought into Presence

At first reading it may seem as though the title of this chapter---the Eleventh Promise---makes no sense. Change *thought* into *presence?* What in the world does *that* mean?

It means, get out of your Mind and into your Soul. When you are in your Mind you are caught up in Thought. When you are in your Soul you are experiencing pure Presence.

Now you might think I am talking here about the Presence of God, but I am not. I am talking about the Presence of You. When you are in your Soul, as opposed to being in your Mind, you are experiencing the pure Presence of You. In this state of pure Presence you want nothing, need nothing, seek nothing, lack nothing, and know everything. You know who you are, where you are, why you are here, and what you intended to do here when you came here. You are clear. There is no confusion, no complexity, no consternation. You are not focused with worldly things except insofar as they serve the purpose of your presence here, which is to announce and to declare, to express and to experience, to become and to fulfill the next grandest version of the greatest vision ever you held about who you are.

Who I am is Divinity Itself, encapsulated, individuated, in the singularization of The Singularity that is, in this incarnation, called Neale. I have come here to express that, to *know that in my own experience.* I wish to know myself experientially, as *well* as conceptually. In the Realm of the Absolute I can know myself conceptually, but I cannot experience myself as what I know myself to be, for in the Realm of the Absolute there is Only The All, Always. That is not an environment made for expression, it is an environment made for compression. In that environment, every moment is compressed into one moment, the Only Moment There Is. In that environment, everything is compressed into one thing, the Only Thing There Is.

The Realm of the Relative was created as an environment in which that which is compressed could be expressed. Indeed, that which we call the physical universe is a model of that dynamic. A pinpoint of incomprehensibly compressed energy exploded, in the Big Bang, into the expression of that same energy in incalculable profusion and infinite diversity.

The One Thing burst wide open to reveal the Many Things It Is.

You are undergoing exactly the same process. You *are* that process, being undergone. You are God "godding." the One Thing exploding. You are the beginning and the end, the Alpha and the Omega, the beginning and the end, the here and the there, the before and the after, the big and the small, the high and the low, the sum and the substance of all that ever was, is now, and ever will be.

> You are the beginning and the end, the Alpha and the Omega, the beginning and the end, the here and the there, the before and the after, the big and the small, the high and the low, the sum and the substance of all that ever was, is now, and ever will be.

You do not know this completely all of the time, although you have occasional glimpses of it some of the time, because if you knew this completely all of the time you would be back in the Realm of the Absolute. Complete Knowing Always is exactly what that Realm is, yet in order to exist outside of that Realm you do not Always Know Everything.

You can know some things all of the time, and all things some of the time, but you cannot know All Things All of the Time. You will step into that again, when you return to the Realm of the Absolute, but here, in the Realm of the Relative, you are happy to know and experience your Self in aggregate parts, so that you may appreciate (that is, grow) all of it over time.

Time itself, of course, does not exist, but is yet another invention of your genius, allowing you to cut up the Single Moment into uncountable smaller units of Itself, through which device you get to experience your Divinity *one thing at a time*.

When all of this is even partially understood, Thought turns into Presence, through a process in which the Mind melds with the Soul and the local self becomes one with the Universal Self.

Inducing a meeting between Mind and Soul

I have been talking a lot here about the Mind collaborating with the Soul, about melding with the Soul, and about embracing the Soul's perspective. Yet for many people the question is, *How do I do this?*

It is not nearly as hard or as mysterious as it may sound. All it takes is a little practice---and some faith in the process. Faith is necessary because at first you may not believe that what is happening is really happening. That is, you might be tempted to call it something else. Like, for instance, your "imagination." Or "wishful thinking." Your Mind, you see, will do everything in its power to keep you from what it imagines to be your abandonment of it. Only after your Mind sees that you are not "leaving for good," but are, in fact, *taking it along with you*, can it relax sufficiently to allow you to journey to the Soul.

It is your Mind's job, remember, to ensure your survival, and if it thinks you are acting in a way that will threaten your ability to make your way through this world, it will do everything in its power to stop you. If it thinks you are starting to "act crazy" with all this talk of "going to the Soul," it will throw up all kinds of barriers to your doing that. You won't even be able to meditate. You won't even be able to pray. Your mind will play snippets of songs in your head, or create itches in your body that jump around all over the place, or make it impossible for you to even sit comfortably. *Anything* to disrupt your journey to the Soul!

Yet we have said repeatedly here and in the text of *When Everything Changes, Change Everything* that the WECCE Technology is not about rejecting the Mind, escaping the Mind, or abandoning the Mind in favor of the Soul. It is about using the Mind *in collaboration* with the Soul.

Up to now you may have been using the Mind *exclusively*, as if it was *the only tool you have*. Now we are going to expand your tool chest, bring in some new data---data available only from that place where the Soul resides. So you *must* take a journey to the Soul.

You can do this, ironically, by going nowhere. You need merely be Here Now, fully. It is your Mind that lives in Yesterday and Tomorrow. Your Soul lives Right Here Right Now, Always. So to get to the Soul, simply *push your focus forward* from any thoughts of the past (like what happened last night, or what annoyed you just a moment ago, or that song from long ago that you can't get out of your mind), then *pull it back* from any thoughts of the future (like what you are worried could happen this year, or what you are supposed to be doing today instead of *this*, or what's on your plate for tomorrow, etc.), and "Be Here Now," as wonderful Ram Dass put it.

There are a lot of ways to do this. Study the pattern in the carpet, scan the colors in the drapes, notice the make of the cars going by your window, count the number of individual sounds you're hearing right now, or just listen to your breath. Close your eyes and just listen to your breath. When you feel yourself being Right Here, Right Now---or as close to being Fully Present as you can get (your Mind will still be hovering on the fringes, trying to tempt you back into Thinking and away from simply Being)---you're ready to conduct this little Experiment, which I'm going to ask you to do several times in the next 24 hours, okay?

Experiment #4
"Don't Mind a Thing"

This should be fun. Today, invite yourself to change the manner in which you live. Just for right now, don't "mind" a thing. Most of us go through life "minding" everything. That is, we are considering it and experiencing it with our Mind. Today, for a little bit here and there, we're going to see if we can consider and experience life from a different perspective.

1. Set an alarm on your phone or watch to go off five times in the next 24 hours. When the alarm sounds, stop whatever you are doing, take a single deep breath, and refocus your Mind away from its thoughts of the past or the future, bringing your full attention to the present moment and to what's Right Here, Right Now.

2. Now, breathing slowly, naturally, and normally---as you might when you are asleep---take a journey to your Soul...which means, *don't go anywhere.* Stay *Right Here*, even though your Mind will desperately try to take you back to Yesterday or Tomorrow. Just keep refocusing on what you're hearing, smelling, feeling, and sensing *right this minute.*

3. Once you feel yourself being Right Here, Right Now, close your eyes (if you have not almost automatically already done so) and open yourself to simple awareness. There is something you know about about your Self in this time and place. Just breathe into that, gently and without any sense of rush or hurry or need. Just breathe into it.

4. From this knowing, enlarge your receptivity to receive a particular message that your Soul has for you Right Now. It may be a word, an image, or a feeling, but it is a particular message, specific to you. Just open yourself to what that message is. It will be right there.

5. Now, to prove to your Mind that you are not abandoning it, invite your Mind to take the Soul's message, whatever it might be (word, image, or feeling, or just a deep awareness), and overlay it on any thought your Mind has been dwelling on recently, having to do with the past or the future. *Add this new data* to the data of your Mind.

6. Good. Now take a deep, cleansing breath---perhaps two---slowly open your eyes, and gently move back into your day. You may feel different, softly detached somehow, but that's perfectly okay. Do this five times today, every time the alarm sounds.

7. You have just learned how to change Thought into Presence. Being fully present as often as you can will cure your Thought Dis-ease.

Chapter Twelve: Change Reaction into Response

You have to understand something. Up until now you have been doing nothing but reacting. What we're going to do now is change Reaction to Response.

What I say you have been doing nothing but reacting, I mean that you have been "acting as you did before." This is called re-acting, or *reenacting*. So when something happens in your life, you reach into your databank and look to see what is going on again (all of life is repetitive) and how you are supposed to act again.

There is nothing "wrong" with this. It is not as if you are doing something "bad." It is just not *getting you anywhere*. You keep going around in circles. You life becomes patterned, your reactions become "grooved." And the older you get, the more "grooved" they become. Pretty soon people around you start finding you quite predictable. They begin putting you in a box, saying that you "always react that way."

This happens to all of us. It's happened to you and it's happened to me. There's not much growth here. More important, there's not much happiness. That's because people who habitually react from their old database find themselves moving more and more into Survival Mode---and that's not a very exciting place to be.

Remember, your Mind's job to make sure you survive. It doesn't care whether you are "happy" or not. It only cares about your being alive. Yet you are *not* alive. You are among the walking dead.

Dr. Elisabeth Kübler-Ross once said that to me, and she shocked me into recognizing what I had fallen into. I was privileged to have met the famed psychiatrist who wrote the book *On Death & Dying* and who practically single-handedly created the hospice movement in this country, and ultimately I worked on her personal staff. And at one point very early in our working relationship I was discussing with her how I had not been very happy for years. She turned to me sharply and said, "How could you be? *You are among the walking dead*."

> **We've been *taught* to be cautious. Heck, some of us have been taught to be *scared*.**

Wow, people don't say things like that very often---I mean, you can go through your whole *life* and not have anyone say something like that to you---so it hit me right between the eyes. Especially coming from a world famous psychiatrist!

I started looking at myself. I began watching how I was living. Once again, a few months later, Elisabeth said to me, "You call that *living*? I call that *dying*."

What I "got" was that I was not doing very much creating in my life, I was simply reacting---doing all the things I had done before....*even though they had gotten me nowhere*. Elisabeth was inviting me (not too gently, either---that was not her way) to take a look at that, and to make "a left turn," as she would put it.

She urged me to stop "coming from yesterday" and stop "fretting about tomorrow" and to "really live." For most people that's a pretty big order. We've been *taught* to be cautious. Heck, some of us have been taught to be *scared*. Scared of all the *what if's* and the *might be's* and the *watch out's*. Scared of our own shadow.

Elisabeth didn't have much patience with Fear, so if you were going to hang around *her* you were going to have to drop that one. Pretty fast. And I did. I learned to turn Fear into Excitement. Yet now I had to learn, as well, to turn Reaction into Response. This required me to get out of my complicated Thoughts and into simple Presence much more often.

It was from Elisabeth, my life's first great teacher (after my Mom and Dad), and, later, from Rev. Terry Cole-Whittaker, my life's second great teacher, that I learned how to get the Mind to simmer down and to find my way to the Present Moment, where the Soul resides.

(It is said that all of us have Three Angels who visit us in our lives. These are people who come to us at pivotal moments and times---perhaps even *creating* those pivotal moments and times---and who bring us something that we absolutely could not have gotten anywhere else, or in any other way. Mine have been Dr. Elisabeth Kübler-Ross, Rev. Terry Cole-Whittaker, and the poet Em Claire (who is now my wife!). There are other "guides" who move us along the way...who maybe even guide us to these angels...and they, too, play incredibly important roles in our lives. You know right now who these Angels and Guides are or have been in your life.}

In the last chapter, we talked about Presence, and how to achieve it. Now let's take a look at how to use Presence to turn Reaction into Response.

In the book on which this Workbook is based there appears a process that I call Notice the Moment. It is a very effective tool, using Pure Presence to produce Creative Response.

- - - - - - ASSIGNMENT #7 - - - - - - -

1. Turn to Page 95 in *When Everything Changes, Change Everything* and read through the Notice the Moment process that makes up Chapter 11. It's a short chapter and will take you just a few minutes.

2. Now please read through the process one more time, while the first reading is still fresh in your mind. I want you to really get into the movement of what is happening here with this lady.

3. In your WECCE Journal, write down your impression of what she went through to get where she got---and where, in fact, you think she *did* get.

4. Now, in your Journal, make a list of five situations, people, or circumstances to which you almost automatically react in a certain way. Be honest with yourself and just make a list of where you feel "grooved," and when your next thought, word, or action is almost predictable.

5. Take one of these five and "run" the Notice the Moment Process on yourself. You can do this in your head, or actually write out a dialogue with yourself on paper.

6. Learn this process until you can go through it backward and forward in your head. Because that's exactly what I'd like you to invite yourself to do the next time you catch yourself Reacting, rather than Responding, to any situation.

Remember that "responding" is the act of creation. "Reacting" is an act of replaying an action that you took once before. By using Presence instead of Thought in typically reactive situations, you open a pathway to the Soul, where an entirely different perspective will be found. And as you know from WECCE, perspective creates perception, perception creates belief, belief creates behavior---and your present behaviors create many of the future events of your life. So if you want to change your life, change Reaction into Response.

Experiment #5
"ReCreation"

The purpose of life, *Conversations with God* says, is to recreate yourself anew in the next golden moment of Now in the next grandest version of the greatest vision ever you held about who you are. One of the fastest ways to do this is to turn Reaction into Response.

1. **Open your WECCE Journal and take a look at the five situations, people, or circumstances to which you almost automatically react in a certain way. Bring them to the front of your Mind (they are by now deeply embedded and you may not even be aware of them in the moments they are presenting themselves) and try to keep them there in the days ahead.**

2. **On a sheet of paper, list these five situations, people, or circumstances in a column down the left-hand side.**

3. **In a second column, after each listing, write down how you would** *like* **to experience yourself in these moments if you thought you could Respond rather than React. What I am inviting you to do here to** *be creative* **and decide upon your Response** *ahead of time.*

4. **Memorize what you put down on that sheet of paper.**

5. **For the next three days, if and whenever these situations, people, or circumstances place themselves in your space, move directly in your Mind to your memory of how you choose to Respond, then step into that.**

6. **When the moment has passed, allow yourself to notice how you did with that. Keep a record of these interactions in your WECCE Journal.**

7. **Do this for six months, making a new list of situations, people, or circumstances when the old list is no longer applicable because your Reality about these situations, people, or circumstances has been "healed." (A healing is anything that brings you back to your True Self.)**

The final promise of the WECCE Technology is that the times of turmoil in your life can turn into times of peace. They can. And will. If you will use the Technology consistently---and if you know one of Life's best kept secrets.

In order for you to change turmoil into peace in your life you will have to change your idea about who you are, where you are, why you are where you are, and what you are trying to do here.

As I said in the WECCE text, these are what I have called Life's Four Fundamental Questions. Most people have never asked themselves these questions, much less answered them. I believe it is vitally important that you do so if you want to live a happy, fulfilling life, because the answer to these questions could dramatically alter your perspective.

It is also important to note that there are no single answers to these questions that are "right." But you must answer the questions, even if your answers change from day to day. The book invites you to respond to those questions. Some time may have passed since you read the book, so here in this Workbook life is going to extend to you an invitation to respond to these questions again. (And remember, it's okay if your responses are different now from what they were a short time ago.)

SPOTLIGHT ON THE SELF

Right now ask yourself, "Who am I?" What is the true essence of my being? What is my true identity? Then ask yourself, "Where am I?" What is this place where I am experiencing life? Now ask: "Why am I here?" Why not be in some other place or realm? Why did God/Life/Me place me here? Is my being here just a biological incident? Finally, ask yourself: What am I intending to do here? What was my original intent in coming to this physical life? Notice your answers to these questions, and how they affect your day-to-day experience.

Life is not nearly as mysterious as some would have us believe. In fact, we can pretty much chart out how it works and how it goes. WECCE does this for us. It tells us that everything starts with Being. On the Clock of Life, Being is at 12 O'clock High. Everything starts there.

What are you "being" right now? Take a look at that. Right now, this minute, as you are reading this, what are you being? Are you being "bored"? Are you being "captivated"? Are you being "restful", "peaceful", "curious," "knowing," "wise"?

Notice that from your place of Being your Perspective will arise. And from that your perception.

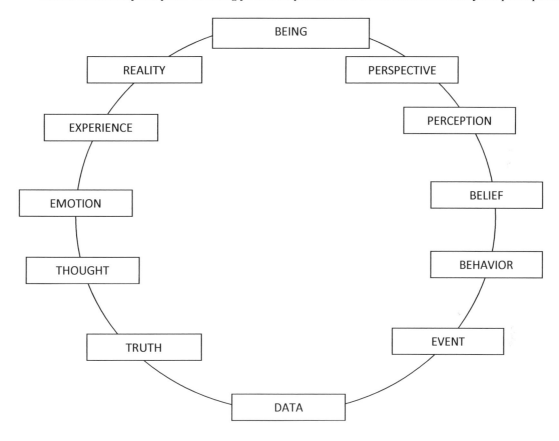

Now follow your Life Clock around and see how perception leads to beliefs, beliefs produce behaviors, behaviors result in events, events place data in your Mind's memory bank, data produces the truth you hold about an event, truth creates a thought about that event, thought generates emotion, emotion gives birth to experience, and your experience creates your reality.

Now---and this is *very* important for you to see (look *closely* at the circle above)---your reality then immediately creates *your next State of Being*. Nervous? Disappointed? Angry? Resentful? Fearful? Anxious? And if you don't pay attention and take control, this new State of Being produces a new perspective, which results in a new perception, which creates a new belief...and soon we're *off to the races!* Life has become a gamble, a roulette wheel. "Round and round and round she goes, where she stops, nobody knows..."

YOU have to stop it. Yet most people don't know how to do that. But you do. Because you have the WECCE Technology.

The Technology tells you that you can control *any one of the elements on this Circle.* You can change any aspect that you wish. Indeed, *you can change them all.* And that's what I am inviting you to do! When everything changes, *change everything.*

That's what the title of the book means! It means celebrate your Self and your own ability to create and experience your reality as you choose---no matter *what* is going on around you.

Remember, exterior events have nothing to do with your interior reality. Yet your interior reality *can* have an effect on exterior events. Did you follow that? Are you with me here? *Your State of Mind creates your Reality,* and your present Reality creates your next State of Being, which in turn creates your perspective, which leads, ultimately, to the events of your life. (Once more, see the circle above.)

> **Your State of Mind creates your Reality, and your present Reality creates your next State of Being.**

To change turmoil into peace, change the *starting point* on your Circle of Life---or what I sometimes call the Life Clock.

Most people begin their creation process at the 5 o'clock spot on the clock...with an Event. That is, their Reality Creation begins when an Event occurs. But when we use the WECCE Technology we start the process of Reality Creation at 12 o'clock high---at the place of Pure Being.

You do this by deciding first what you *choose* to Be *before* an event occurs.

ONE IF LIFE'S BEST KEPT SECRETS:
Events are completely predictable

Now you might say, "How can I decide ahead of time what I choose to be, how can I do this before an event happens, if I don't know what events are *going* to happen?"

But the fact is, you *do* know what's going to happen! Did you know that? There are virtually no surprises in life. Nearly all events are repeats or "re-runs" of previous events, viewed from the perspective of their *Energy Content*---and Energy Content is the only thing that the Soul is concerned with. Everything else is Form, not Content. The *form* of your life's event may change from day to day or year to year, but the *content* will be virtually the same across your entire lifetime.

Let me give you an example of what I mean.

Here are three events: (A) Partner is found to be having an affair; (B) Business associate is embezzling money from the company account; (C) Political candidate changes his entire platform after you vote him into office.

All three of these events are different in terms of form. If you encountered one of these experiences you might say, "That's never happened to me before." In truth, however, these three events are identical. Their form is different, but their Energy Content is the same. That is, the *feeling* is the same.

In each case you feel...

...can you think of the word....?

Try....."betrayed."

The Energy Content here is called Betrayal.

There is virtually no new Energy Content introduced into your life after the first few years. You may think that you are having all kinds of new experiences, but in truth you are simply encountering old experiences in new forms.

To prove this to yourself, try this little Exercise...

Exercise 7

1. **On the chart below, match the Energy Content from the list that follows** (ANGER, LOVE, FEAR, JOY, FRUSTRATION) **with the Events in the left column, plac-ing the content description that best fits the Event in the column at right. Use only the words in the Energy Content list. Match as good as you can.**

EVENT	ENERGY CONTENT
Spouse hugs and kisses you and then makes love with you	
You rock your 1-year-old grandchild in your arms	
The keys to your car are nowhere to be found	
The price of your dinner is twice what you expected	
The car just ran out of gas	
You've won $1,000 in the Lottery	
A man cuts you off in traffic, nearly sending you off the road	
The hotel has lost your reservation and you've been traveling all night	
A thief pulls you into an alley and points a gun at you	
You got the job!	
You got laid off	
The theatre tickets were left at home	
A window pane is heard being broken in your house at 3 a.m.	
Your soufflé has turned out just right	
There's a 100-foot drop-off on the passenger side of the car	
Your feet are killing you and your sweetie gives you a foot massage	
A man in the bank shouts "Everybody on the floor, this is a robbery!"	
Your dog jumps up and cuddles into your lap, looking up at you	
The painters put the wrong color in the dining room	
You just bought a new car	

2. Notice how many of the events in the left hand column are identical.
3. Notice how many of the words in the right column are identical.

The exercise above demonstrates that you cannot predict the form of the Events that are going to occur in your life, but you can be very sure that the Energy Content of your life's Events *will be repetitive*, and thus, *predictable*. You *know* that before a month is out, *something* is going to occur that produces in you anger, love, fear, joy, or frustration, among a host of other emotions. This is Energy Content, and there is no new Energy Content left that you have not experienced.

Yet now here is a remarkable revelation: Energy Content can be *changed*. This is because *you are supplying this content.*

Most people believe that it is the Event that holds such content, but, in fact, Events are simply happenings, occurrences, that carry neutral energy. Nothing has any meaning save the meaning you give it. When you give it meaning, you give it energy. That's why, when something negative happens, many people will say, "Just don't give it any energy…"

Knowing that Energy Content can be changed saves you from repeating over and over again the negative emotional patterns that have run your life. I am now going to give you a startling example of that, from the life of Byron Katie.

Yes, you can!

Now, again, you may take the position that it is not possible to change your choice of emotions, which is Change #2 in the list on Pg 3 of this Workbook, but, in fact, you can. You can do this by altering the Energy Content that you overlay on any Event.

Byron Katie, you will remember, is the author of *Loving What Is*. I consider her to be at a level very near mastery in the living of her life. In her writings she tells the story of how one day she was accosted while walking down a city street and pulled into an alley. I'm paraphrasing it her as best as I can remember it. There, a man pointed a gun at her, told her to give him all her money, then said, "I'm sorry, but you've gotten too good a look at me. I'm going to have to kill you."

Now you might recognize this as one of the Events in the Exercise above (it's the 9th one down). Check to see what Energy Content you posted next to the item in the chart. I wouldn't be surprised if it was FEAR or ANGER. Interestingly, in Katie's case it was neither. It was LOVE. She said she simply looked with compassion at the man and said, "Do the best you can do. If that's the best you can do in this situation, do the best you can do."

The thief gave her a quizzical look, trying to figure out where she was "coming from" which such a remark, saw that she was not at all scared, apparently got scared himself at the thought of who such a person might be, dropped his gun *and* her money and simply ran off, shaking his head.

> **Masters are those who choose *ahead of time* how they are going to respond to any given event.**

Katie changed the Energy Content of this Event even as it was taking place. It's even easier to do that *after* an Event has occurred. And masters are those who do it *before* an Event occurs.

They do this by deciding *ahead of time* how they are going to be Responding (as opposed to Reacting) the next time an Event with perfectly predictable Energy Content occurs.

I alternately call this Energy Content the "Energy Package" with which an Event is often delivered to you by your Mind. A very wise man once said to me, "Anyone can deliver a package to your door, but they can't force you to open the door and take it into your house."

When Life delivers an Event wrapped in an Energy Package to your door, you do not have to take it in. You can unwrap the package and take the Event inside, leaving the packaging right where it is. You can even re-wrap the Event in the package of your choice.

Masters do this *before the package arrives*, because they *know* that it's *going* to arrive. And how do they know this? *Because they ordered it.* That's right. They ordered it from the Life Store.

Masters are those who know that every life Event has been called TO them BY them, precisely for this *reason*. Precisely so that they may practice expressing and experiencing themselves as who they have decided ahead of time to be in circumstances of varying energies.

They have made what I call the Next Time Choice. Theirs is an amazing process. And *you can do the same thing.* You can practice Mastery in Living.

Exercise 8

1. **On the chart below, write in the Energy Content that you wish to overlay on the Events in the left column. Use any word that you wish to describe how you are now choosing to feel, ahead of time, if and when the events below should occur in your life.**

EVENT	YOUR CHOICE OF ENERGY CONTENT
Spouse hugs and kisses you and then makes love with you	
You rock your 1-year-old grandchild in your arms	
The keys to your car are nowhere to be found	
The price of your dinner is twice what you expected	
The car just ran out of gas	
You've won $1,000 in the Lottery	
A man cuts you off in traffic, nearly sending you off the road	
The hotel has lost your reservation and you've been traveling all night	
A thief pulls you into an alley and points a gun at you	
You got the job!	
You got laid off	
The theatre tickets were left at home	
A window pane is heard being broken in your house at 3 a.m.	
Your soufflé has turned out just right	
There's a 100-foot drop-off on the passenger side of the car	
Your feet are killing you and your sweetie gives you a foot massage	
A man in the bank shouts "Everybody on the floor, this is a robbery!"	
Your dog jumps up and cuddles into your lap, looking up at you	
The painters put the wrong color in the dining room	
You just bought a new car	

2. Notice how many of the events in the left hand column are identical.
3. Notice how many of the words in the right column are positive, and thus, life enhancing and how many are negative, and thus, life detracting.

Using the Next Time Choice process, you can turn any time of turmoil into a time of peace. Remember, "turmoil" is the package an Event comes in. You can re-wrap it in "peace" whenever you wish.

Afterword

I consider the WECCE Technology to be one of the most important social-spiritual-psychological tools we could ever have been given. I hope you will use this Workbook in conjunction with the Main Text, and that you will consult that text often. It is a remarkable combination of modern psychology and contemporary spirituality that has already helped thousands. You cannot read *When Everything Changes, Change Everything* enough.

Nor can you read the *Conversations with God* books enough. The nine books in that series, and the 15 books that have followed and that are extensions of them (such as *Neale Donald Walsch's LITTLE BOOK OF LIFE),* can dramatically change your experience, and hence, your reality. I know this because I have received thousands of letters and emails (that number is not exaggerated) from readers telling me so.

I hope you will take a look at the entire CwG Cosmology, including the *Conversations with God COMPANION,* a wonderful workbook centering on the messages of the Original Trilogy. As I have said repeatedly, it is not enough to simply read one or two of the books. CwG was meant to be a major work, and a major study opportunity for those seeking a new way of being human.

If you have an interest in receiving spiritual mentoring, I work with a handful of people every year for a period of three months to assist and empower them, using direct personal interaction by telephone. For more information, check out the Spiritual Mentoring Program by following this link:

http://www.nealedonaldwalsch.com/index.php?p=Doc&c=mentor

And finally, if you would like to learn about how you can spend five days with me in residence in my own home in Ashland, Oregon with just 12 people, engaging in ongoing and very personal conversation around all of the *Conversations with God* material, my experience, and your own life and how it can change...write to:

neale@nealedonaldwalsch.com

Ask about **The Homecoming: 5 Days in Residence with Neale**, offered twice each year at my home.

I hope you have found this Workbook helpful as you seek to learn more and more about the WECCE Technology. I want to again---yes, one *more* time---urge you to return over and over to the original text. Study it deeply. Then re-read this Workbook. Keep coming back to all of this material until it becomes second nature to you.

I promise you, it can be transformative.

Love and hugs, and blessings on your journey...

Neale.